IN SEARCH OF
SOLUTIONS

A Norton Professional Book

IN SEARCH OF
SOLUTIONS

A NEW DIRECTION
IN PSYCHOTHERAPY

BILL O'HANLON
MICHELE WEINER-DAVIS

W. W. Norton & Company
New York • London

Production Manager: Leeann Graham
Manufacturing by Haddon Craftsmen, Inc.

Library of Congress Cataloging-in-Publication Data

O'Hanlon, William Hudson.
In search of solutions : a new direction in psychotherapy / Bill O'Hanlon,
Michele Weiner-Davis
    p.   cm.
"A Norton professional book."
Includes bibliographical references and index.
ISBN 0-393-70437-8 (pbk.)
    1. Solution-focused therapy.   I. Weiner-Davis, Michele.   II. Title.
RC489.P68O33   2003
616.89'14—dc21   2003059533

W. W. Norton & Company, Inc., 500 Fifth Avenue, New York, N.Y. 10110
www.wwnorton.com

W. W. Norton & Company, Ltd., Castle House, 75/76 Wells St., London
W1T 3QT

1   3   5   7   9   0   8   6   4   2

To Steffanie for being the solution I was searching for. And to my father, Robert Edward O'Hanlon, who loved to read and would have been proud to know that I had written a book.

—B. O'H.

To my supportive husband, Jim, whose extraordinary patience and expert advice help to make this vision a reality. To Danielle, whose question, "Mom, are you done with this book yet?" now has an acceptable answer. To Zachary, who has helped to keep my life balanced. To my father, who taught me about ambition. And to my mother, who has been inspirational in too many ways to mention.

—M. W.-D.

Contents

Preface to Paperback Edition

It is hard to believe it has been 15 years since this book was first published.

Bill first came across Michele's work in an obscure newsletter, where she had written about a case in which she had followed a solution- rather than pathology- or explanation-oriented path. He admired her writing and what she had done in the case ("The Path Not Taken") that had appeared in Steve de Shazer's newsletter/journal, *The Underground Railroad*, in 1986. At the next American Association of Marriage and Family Therapists (AAMFT) conference, Bill asked de Shazer about Michele. De Shazer said that Michele was the best clinician that had been through their training program and was now "part of the team." Bill was impressed, especially because he rarely, if ever, heard Steve say anything complimentary about other therapists (he has never heard him say anything complimentary about another therapist since that time, either).

Bill and Michele met up later at the AAMFT conference and found that they enjoyed one another's company. Before each headed home, Bill said to Michele, "Let's write a book together." Michele laughed and readily agreed. On the plane flight home, Bill wrote an outline for the book. He called Michele when he got home and told her he already had an outline and would send it to her. Michele was astonished. She had thought Bill was joking about the book.

When she was assured that Bill was not joking, Michele asked, "Why would you want to write a book with me?" (Her self-esteem is a tad better these days.) Bill told her that she was a great writer, she had good case examples, and he was looking for someone to help him articulate this emerging way of working in therapy that he was calling *solution-oriented therapy*. That clinched the partnership that led to the publication of *In Search of Solutions* and began a fruitful collegial relationship that has spanned these 15 years.

Our most prominent memory in writing this book is of laughing and laughing. We both enjoy humor and the situation in which we wrote together made the process of collaboration even more humorous. Back in the late 1980s we were both techno-peasants and had only early computer models — Bill had an Apple II computer and Michele had one of the first Macintoshes. Because of our technological backwardness, there was no easy way to exchange files. We eventually found a way to connect the computers over the phone line but, once we began to exchange our writing in digital form, we were dismayed to see the transferred text appear on our screens one letter at a time. Michele actually fell asleep one night at her computer waiting for the text to come in. (The fact that we used late-night phone calls — due to high long-distance rates in those days — also encouraged her slumber.) We could have written the book in half the time if only our computers had cooperated.

But we laughed when the text came in with many extra carriage returns that it took us hours to fix. We laughed when we got together and watched tapes of each other's work. We laughed and laughed; and we learned and learned. Gradually the outlines of this new direction began to come clear. The result is in this book.

In Search of Solutions has been translated into many different languages and has been used as a textbook for many courses. Now, some 15 years later, this once-radical material has become part of the mainstream. We are happy to have it available in paperback form for the first time.

Bill O'Hanlon
Michele Weiner-Davis
June 2003

Acknowledgements

Thanks and acknowledgement go to family, friends, and colleagues who made significant contributions to the text: Dan Dunne, Pat Hudson, Tony Heath, Angie Hexum, Sandy Kutler, Paul Lambakis, and Terry Moore. Also, thanks goes to Deborah Malmud and Michael McGandy who shepherded this new edition through publication.

Bill would like especially to acknowledge our editor, Susan Barrows (now Munro). Because Bill had a talented coauthor, Susan was able to put away the "Barrows's machete" that she had to use for one of his earlier books and use only her "Barrows' razor" this time.

Michele would like to thank the supportive staff as YSB for providing her with rich clinical experiences while teaming, practicing, and supervising solution-oriented therapy. Arnold Woodruff deserves special gratitude from Michele both for being a constant source of intellectual stimulation and for being a dear friend. She is indebted to the staff of the Brief Family Therapy Center for influencing her thinking during the years of her association with them. In particular, she appreciates her friendship with Eve Lipchik and her association with Steve de Shazer, who taught her to be simple minded and challenged her to "take all this further or else."

Introduction

This book offers a new way to think about and approach therapy. It is a method that focuses on people's competence rather than their deficits, their strengths rather than their weaknesses, their possibilities rather than their limitations.

One of the pioneers of this approach was the late psychiatrist, Milton Erickson. One of his cases is a nice illustration of using solution-oriented therapy.

Erickson once worked with a woman called "Ma" (Rossi, 1980, Vol. 1, pp. 197–201), who had always wanted to learn to read and write but had never been able to overcome her block to these goals. She was not given the chance to acquire these skills when young, and at age 16 she resolved that she would learn. At the age of 20, she hit upon the idea of taking in teachers as boarders and having them teach her to read and write. In the years that followed, her boarders and then her children relentlessly tried to teach her, all to no avail. She would become frightened and go blank whenever anyone tried to explain reading and writing to her.

At the age of 70, still unable to read, she came in contact with Erickson. He promised her that she would be reading and writing within three weeks and that he would ask her to do nothing that she did not already know how to do. She was skeptical but intrigued. First, he asked her to pick up a pencil. He told her to pick it up any haphazard fashion, as a baby would. Next he asked her to make some marks on a paper, any scribbling marks, as a baby unable to write might do. Then he asked her to make some straight lines, as she would do on a board that she wanted to saw or as she would in a garden when she wanted to plant a straight row. She could make the lines up and down or across or diagonally. Then she was to draw some donut holes and then draw the two halves of a donut when it is broken in half. Then she was to draw the two sides of a gabled roof. He continued to instruct her to make these marks and to practice them. She practiced although she did not see its relevance.

At the next session Erickson told her that the only difference between a pile of lumber and a house was that the latter was merely put together. She agreed to this, but again did not see the relevance. With Erickson's guidance, she put those marks together to make all the letters of the alphabet. When she had completed that, Erickson let her in on the fact that she had just learned to write all the letters. Spelling words was merely a matter of putting letters together, he told her. After getting her to put the letters together, he told her that she now knew how to form words. Erickson got her to name certain words because each word has a name, just like each farm animal has a name. Gradually he maneuvered her into writing a sentence and had her name all the words in it. The sentence read, "Get going Ma and put some grub on the table." When she said this aloud, she realized it was just like talking (her late husband had often used this phrase). The translation into reading was easily made within a three week period.

Bill remembers the first case in which he (somewhat by accident) used the solution orientation presented in this book.

He had just started working in a mental health center when a former client of another therapist sought help on an emergency basis. The woman's therapist was on vacation and Bill had time available, so he agreed to see the woman. Not wanting to interfere with what the other therapist would be doing when she returned, Bill was cautious. He asked the woman what had brought her this particular day and whether this was related to what she had seen the other therapist about previously. The woman reported that she had seen the other therapist about being depressed for about a year and that they had stopped doing therapy some time ago because she had overcome the depression.

Bill then asked how she had learned to overcome the depression. The woman proceeded to give a detailed description of several strategies she and the other therapist had come up with to enable her to avoid sinking into depression when she started to feel down. These included calling a friend on the telephone, going for rides on her bicycle and making sure that she continued her regular activities, like going to college and work. She brightened considerably while discussing these ideas. Bill asked her if she thought those things would work for her now. She replied that she thought they would, but that she had forgotten them until he asked. She ended up telling Bill that she now knew that she did not have to be in therapy to solve her problem, but she also recognized that if she had not come in, she would have gone into a deep depression. The interview had lasted 20 minutes. Bill had done brief therapy for some time, but 20 minutes was even more brief than he had thought therapy could be! When the other therapist returned from her vacation several weeks later, she made a follow-up call to her ex-client and found that she was getting along fine, with no recurrence of the depression.

A case of Michele's shows yet another facet of this solution orientation.

A couple came to see Michele because of their three-year-old "monster." Janet, the mother, immediately assured Michele that their daughter Mindy was not like other three-year-olds. Janet was an educated woman in her thirties who read every parenting article or book she could get her hands on. She was confident that Mindy's obnoxious behavior far exceeded the limits of normal "terrible threes." She indicated that Mindy nagged all time, never took "no" for an answer, constantly interrupted adults, threw temper tantrums with no provocation, pinched her baby sister when unsupervised and refused to go to bed in the evening. (The list of complaints was actually much longer.)

This little girl had the family turned upside down. Janet felt certain that her lack of parenting skills caused Mindy's intolerable behavior. Not only did Janet feel inadequate, but she also felt extremely guilty for not experiencing feelings of love toward Mindy much of the time, something she felt that all good mothers do. To make matters worse, Mindy behaved appropriately in the presence of others and received a great deal of attention from them, further convincing Janet that she was the cause of the problem. This, in turn, intensified Janet's feelings of inadequacy and alienation.

Ken, the father, was also concerned about their "monster," particularly because he felt bombarded with negative reports about her as soon as he entered the door at the day's end. He also came home for lunch every day, an act of either bravery or masochism since he was barraged with the details of the Mindy-Janet war while he ate. He felt that the marriage was suffering due to the fact that their only topic of conversation was Mindy. He missed the fun times he and Janet used to have together.

During the first session it was quite a feat to help the couple interrupt their litany of complaints and focus on a starting place. However, Janet made an offhand comment that suggested a possible beginning. She reported that she was able to tell what kind of day she would have with Mindy just by the way the child got up in the morning. Michele was eager to explore this further.

Janet explained that every morning she would be awakened by Mindy's voice calling, "Mommy, I'm up." To Janet's ear, sometimes Mindy sounded cheerful when she bellowed out her good morning greeting, while at other times she sounded whiny. Depending on how Janet assessed Mindy's voice, it would determine the type of greeting Mindy received in return. If Mindy sounded cheerful to her, Janet knew they would have a good day. At those times, she would walk into Mindy's room and begin the little routine ditty they had created together: "How is Mommy's little girl?" "I'm fine." "Who loves Mindy?" "Mommy does." Janet and Mindy would then spend a few moments together before going downstairs for breakfast. Typically, the rest of the day was relatively peaceful.

If Mindy sounded whiny to Janet, she would go to Mindy's room with apprehension and anger, and she would not initiate their little song. Of course, Mindy would then confirm Janet's predictions and begin whining, which marked the beginning of a battle-filled day.

Michele asked Janet if she would do an experiment. She suggested that whether Mindy woke up cheerful or grouchy, Janet was to walk into Mindy's room pretending that Mindy was cheerful. This meant that Janet was to have a smile on her face and immediately break into their song regardless of Mindy's mood. Janet immediately thought that this was an interesting idea and was willing to try it.

The next week the couple reported a better week with Mindy. She seemed to have settled down and was more enjoyable to be around. Janet and Ken discussed the positive effects this had on their relationship — more relaxed times and even some laughter. What shocked them the most was *that, although Mindy's behavior was far from perfect, she had mysteriously toilet trained herself completely that week!*

Several sessions later, while we were reviewing their progress before ending treatment, Janet reported that the morning experiment was a real turning point for her. She recognized that she could keep things moving in the right direction despite Mindy's challenges. Furthermore, Janet and Ken had successfully applied this idea to other difficult situations with Mindy.

A MEGATREND

Several years ago, in *Megatrends*, John Naisbitt detailed some sweeping trends that he saw emerging in our society — trends that were perhaps not obvious to others. In a similar manner, we have observed a "megatrend" in psychotherapy. Stated simply, the trend is away from explanations, problems, and pathology, and towards solutions, competence, and capabilities. In the following pages, we articulate and detail this emerging approach so that therapists can use it in their work. We do this by first giving a general overview of the basis for this approach and discussing how it differs from traditional therapy approaches. Then, through an examination of specific principles and the use of case material, we offer some guidelines for putting these ideas into practice.

A Focus on Solutions and Strengths:
An Emerging Trend in Therapy

> It is a way of thinking that doesn't begin by attacking the problem but by seeking solutions — however big or distant that may seem to be — then figuring out how to get there. It is a way of thinking that raises up images of what might be — should be — and thereby helps people see potential

that otherwise might not be understood and evokes action that otherwise might not occur. These images generate energy and forestall early compromise with lesser results. Such images are often dismissed as visionary and impractical, through a state of mind that is one of the burdens of our society. It is a state of mind that operates out of the belief that significant changes cannot — will not — occur. It is a state of mind that inhibits movement toward valid and important goals by discounting them in advance as unachievable. It is a state of mind that too often keeps us chained to the present, as if the present were nearly the best we can hope for. (Rouse, 1985, p. 12)

In the 1960s Abraham Maslow decided that psychology had been moving in the wrong direction. Almost from the start, most psychological inquiries had explored and tried to understand the nature of emotional, behavioral, and psychological *pathology* in human beings. Maslow said that instead we should be studying the best, healthiest specimens of human beings to learn what we want to know about people.

In a similar vein, psychotherapy has for most of its history focused on studying and trying to eliminate people's problems and pathology. There is, however, an emerging trend — a shift in focus from pathology and deficits to strengths, capabilities, and resources in therapy. There is also a move away from searching for *the* explanation for the person's difficulties, for *the real* problem, to looking for solutions that will work for the particular individual, couple, or family seeking therapy.

Therapists often disagree about what causes problems, but there is more agreement about solutions. This has given rise to what is called "technical eclecticism" in the field of psychotherapy. For example, many therapists use such techniques as systematic desensitization from behavior therapy, but have little allegiance to the behavioral model; in fact, they might find behaviorism quite objectionable. Not wish-

ing to argue with success, therapists seem willing to borrow
from outside their primary models for successful interventions from other models.

Perhaps we are too optimistic in calling this emerging
trend a megatrend. In reality, we might simply say that there
is evidence for this shift in many places. However, we write
about the megatrend in an effort to contribute to its creation. In response to the widely discussed question, "Does the
media simply report the news or create it?" we maintain that
it does both. Therefore, we are excited about the prospects
of being instrumental in transforming this trend into a
megatrend.

A BEGINNER'S MIND

We like the Zen saying, "In the beginner's mind there are
many possibilities; in the expert's mind there are few" (Suzuki, 1970). Adopting this attitude in our work, we find it to be
conducive to continually learning new things. Our clients
perpetually teach us how to work with them and how to help
solve their dilemmas. We have yet to find a formula that
captures the diversity of human beings.

This book is no different. While we offer our views on
how to make therapy work, we are aware that we do not have
The Answer to every therapeutic dilemma. From our experience we are confident, however, that the approach we offer
here is successful for the majority of people who seek our
help in therapy.

We ask that you, the reader, approach this material with a
beginner's mind. Some of the things we write might challenge some of your long-held and cherished assumptions
about therapy. We have spent many years unlearning some
"basic" assumptions about problems and psychotherapy. We
often think of the research showing that people about to
enter graduate studies in psychology tend to be "naturally

therapeutic." When tested at the end of their graduate studies, however, they seem to have fewer of these skills. Five years after completing their studies, their natural skills return.

When we teach this material in workshops, we are often approached by clinicians who tell us that they have been doing many of the things we discuss intuitively, but feel better having them validated by some theory and expert. With this book we hope to stimulate your "beginner's mind" and your natural therapeutic abilities.

Finally, it would be a good idea to keep in mind a story that we heard, one which always reminds us that nobody has the definitive answer or final solution to all of human dilemmas.

There was once a man who gave a class for parents on how to parent. He called it, "Ten Commandments for Parents," and parents, being insecure about their abilities, came from far and near to attend his class and learn how to be better parents. At this time he was not married and had no children. One day he met the woman of his dreams and got married. In time they had a child. He then retitled his class, "Five Suggestions for Parents." In time they were blessed with another offspring. He then renamed the class, "Three Tentative Hints for Parents." After their third child was born, he stopped teaching the class altogether.

1.

The Evolution of Psychotherapy
From Explanations and Problems to Solutions

Therapy was spawned in a sea of different disciplines, with tributaries from psychology, medicine and philosophy. These disciplines typically concern themselves with explaining, diagnosing, and understanding human nature. While these disciplines are worthwhile endeavors, time has shown, and we have come more and more to suspect, that therapy involves a set of concerns different from those provided by them. In our view, therapy involves deliberate attempts to produce a change in viewpoint and/or action leading to solution. As many clients can demonstrate, having a good explanation about the nature and origin of the problem does not necessarily produce the desired therapeutic outcome.

Psychoanalysis is, of course, the archetypal approach emphasizing insight to produce change. Occasionally, it does indeed produce results, but more often it leads to situations like that of Alby Singer (Woody Allen) in *Annie Hall*. Soon after they meet, Alby tells Annie that he has been in analysis for 13 years. When she expresses amazement, he quickly

10

counters by telling her that he intends to give it 20 years and go to Lourdes if he has not gotten better by then. Most would agree that there must be a way to ensure that therapy ends successfully in less time than that!

Recently, therapy has emerged as a separate and distinct discipline practiced very often by those outside the formal fields of psychiatry and psychology — social workers, family therapists, ministers, nurses, counselors, and others. Perhaps the presence of these other practitioners has been an impetus for the trend toward seeking change and solutions rather than understanding and explanation.

It has become evident that there are various ways to do effective therapy. However, advocates of different methods and schools often hold diametrically opposed views about the crucial elements and techniques involved in successful therapy. Witness the Evolution of Psychotherapy conference held in Phoenix in December 1985. The faculty members for that conference represented a number of major schools and approaches to therapy and yet little agreement on assumptions or working methods was evident in the presentations (Zeig, 1987). Some might think this is bad news, but we think it is good. There is no one right theory of psychotherapy. Many different theories and many different techniques and approaches seem to produce change and positive results.

Instead of looking for the right theory of therapy, we should perhaps be searching in another direction. Thomas Peters and Robert Waterman had the right idea when they wrote *In Search of Excellence: Lessons from America's Best-Run Companies.* Together they researched a number of the most successful companies in the United States and extrapolated several key ingredients of effective management. They were looking at the most successful, rather than the least successful, cases, at solutions rather than problems.

THE EVOLUTION OF
A SOLUTION ORIENTATION

Traditionally therapy was oriented primarily to the past, searching in the client's childhood for the roots of present symptoms. Then, in the 1960s, with the emergence of behavior therapy, ego psychology, gestalt therapy, family therapy, etc., the present or the "here and now" became a central focus in therapy. Past-oriented therapy was dismissed as time-wasting and too speculative by adherents of these brash new approaches. The new approaches were contemporary, concerned with the generation or maintenance of the symptom in the present, with data that could be confirmed in the present.

Now therapy is evolving beyond this "here and now" orientation to a *future* orientation that is unconcerned with how problems arose or even how they are maintained, but instead is concerned with how they will be solved. From the sea of psychology, medicine and philosophy, we emerge onto the dry land of intervention. In intervention-land there is no right or wrong diagnosis, no right or wrong theory, just data about what works or is useful in particular cases.

A major aspect of this megatrend is a focus on clients' strengths and abilities, in our view a more humane, less painful way to help people change than the old focus on deficits. Several prominent leaders in the family therapy field have noticed this trend as well:

> The orientation of family therapists toward "constructing a reality" that highlights deficits is therefore being challenged. Family therapists are finding that an exploration of strengths is essential to challenge family dysfunctions. The work of Virginia Satir, with its emphasis on growth, is oriented toward a search for normal alternatives. So is the work of Ivan Nagy, with its emphasis on positive connotations and his exploration of the family

value system. Carl Whitaker's technique of challenging
the positions of family members and introducing role dif-
fusion springs from his belief that out of this therapeuti-
cally induced chaos the family members can discover la-
tent strength. Jay Haley and Cloe Madanes' view that the
symptom is organized to protect the family and Mara
Selvini-Palazzoli's paradoxical interventions all point toward family strengths. . . .

In Milton Erickson's work with individuals, he ad-
dressed himself consistently to the "fact" that individuals
have a reservoir of wisdom learned and forgotten but still
available. He suggested that his patients explore alternative ways of organizing their experience without exploring
the etiology or dynamics of the dysfunction. This search
for valid and functional alternatives of transaction is also
applicable in family therapy, for the family is a system that
has available a larger repertory of ways of organizing experience than those it ordinarily uses. One strategy is therefore to bypass an exploration of the historical underpin-
nings of dysfunctional transactions and to take a shortcut
of exploring other, more complex modes of transacting
that promise healthier functioning. . . . (Minuchin and
Fishman, 1981, pp. 268-269)

The approach we offer here was not developed in a vacu-
um. We were influenced by many people over the years.
When we started to articulate this solution orientation, we
noticed that there were other therapists who were on the
same or parallel trails. Although we do not necessarily agree
with all of their views, some aspects of their work seem to be
leading towards or are compatible with a solution-oriented
approach. We see this as evidence that other therapies are
developing more in the direction of solutions rather than
explanations.

Jay Haley (1976) and Thomas Szasz (1961) have given us
the idea that it is best to treat people as if they are normal,

because when people are treated as normal they tend to act more normally. They also made clear the debilitating effects of psychiatric labels. Haley and Richard Rabkin (1977) were among the first to write about the negotiability of the problem definition, an idea we will detail in Chapter 3 (see also Fish, 1973, and O'Hanlon and Wilk, 1987). Bandler and Grinder (1979) have emphasized getting clear outcome images and information as a technique for creating those outcomes.

Among our forerunners the most influential were Milton Erickson, the Mental Research Institute's Brief Therapy Clinic (hereafter referred to as MRI), and the Brief Family Therapy Center (or BFTC). Both the MRI and BFTC groups have been influenced by Erickson's work.

Milton Erickson: An Uncommon Therapist

Erickson was a seminal figure in several areas of therapy: hypnosis, family therapy, brief therapy, and strategic therapy. To this, we can now add another: solution-oriented therapy. Erickson was an unusual figure for his time. He practiced therapy from the late 1920s until the late 1970s. During much of that time, psychoanalysis held sway in psychotherapy; Erickson, however, found his own method of doing therapy far from the mainstream of analysis. When Haley started to observe and study different therapists, he found that Erickson's approach was not only brief, a unique feature in itself, but quite different from anything around at the time (Haley, 1963, 1967, 1973, 1985). In fact, Erickson had been baffling students and observers for many years and continued to do so until his death. Haley has said that, even after spending a number of years intensively studying Erickson's work, "Not a day passes that I do not use something that I learned from Erickson in my work. Yet his basic ideas I only partially grasp. I feel that if I understood more fully what Erickson was trying to explain about changing people, new innovations in therapy would open up before me" (1982, p. 5).

Part of the difficulty in understanding Erickson is that he had no theory—no theory of psychopathology, that is. He speculated very little on the origin of problems. He considered Freud a genius for unraveling the intricacies of the human mind and psychopathology, but hopeless when it came to helping individuals change. Perhaps this distinction makes Erickson's work easier to grasp. He was a genius at helping people change, but he had little expertise or interest in understanding how they became stuck. In fact, Erickson viewed the things that other therapists saw as "psychopathology" as skills, "mental mechanisms" that could be used to create healing as well as problems. He readily used amnesia, hallucinations and other "pathological" states and experiences as therapy techniques, turning what seemed like liabilities into assets. For instance, when Erickson was treating a young man with little self-confidence who had just obtained a job in a bank, he questioned him in some detail about his work, taking particular interest in mistakes he had made. Erickson commented, "Every time he made a mistake in his work, what interested me *always* was the procedure by which it was corrected—never the details of how he made the error." By emphasizing the young man's corrections, he was using his mistakes as a way to help him build his self-confidence (Haley, 1985, Vol. 1, pp. 83–84).

Some time ago, a colleague asked Bill which aspects of Erickson's work would make a lasting contribution to therapy. Bill unhesitatingly replied, "the utilization approach." Erickson held the view that the therapist should, like a good organic gardener, use everything that the client presented— even things that looked like weeds—as part of the therapy. The "weeds" of "resistance," symptoms, rigid beliefs, compulsive behavior, etc., were essential components to be taken into consideration and actively used as part of the solution. In line with this, Erickson thought that therapy should be adjusted to meet the styles and idiosyncrasies of each client.

Erickson told a story to illustrate this utilization approach. When he was in high school, he used to regularly mispronounce a few words. One of them was *government*, which he used to pronounce "goverment." His debate teacher tried in vain to get him to hear and reproduce the correct pronunciation. Finally, she stumbled on an approach that worked. She wrote the name of one of his fellow students on the board, "LaVerne." Erickson could readily pronounce her name correctly. Then she combined her name with government, making it "goLaVernement." Again, Erickson found this within his capability. Lastly, she had him drop the "La." Erickson realized in a flash how to correctly pronounce the word (Rossi, 1980, Vol. 1, p. 110).

Erickson viewed clients as having within them or within their social systems the resources to make the changes they needed to make. The therapist's job is to access these resources and help clients put them to use in the appropriate areas of their lives. Erickson didn't view people as fundamentally flawed or in need of fixing. To Erickson, therapy " . . . was predicated upon the assumption that there is a strong normal tendency for the personality to adjust if given an opportunity" (Rossi, 1980, Vol. 4, p. 505).

Erickson also stressed the importance of respecting the abilities of the client. " . . . (Y)ou ought to rely on the capacity of the individual patient to furnish you the cues and the information by which to organize your psychotherapy. Because the patient can if you give him an opportunity" (Erickson, 1966). He believed that therapy could be accomplished very quickly. "Illness can come on all of a sudden; one can make a massive response all at once to a particular thing. I do not think we need to presuppose or propound some long, drawn-out causation and a long, drawn-out therapeutic process. You see, if illness can occur suddenly, then therapy can occur quite as suddenly" (Rossi, Ryan, and Sharp, 1983, p. 71). He emphasized the role of positive expectations in affecting a cure. " . . . (W)e ought to *expect* to find solutions rather than passively accepting a decree of 'uncurable.' Such an attitude of expectancy is far more conducive to our task of exploration, discovery and healing" (Rossi, 1980, Vol. 2, p. 202).

Erickson developed a technique (later called by de Shazer the "crystal ball technique") that is the first purely solution-oriented technique of which we are aware. Using hypnosis, he helped people create a sense of time distortion, so that they could readily go back and forth in time. He called this "pseudo-orientation in time" (Rossi, 1980, Vol. 4, pp. 397–423). After they were adept at time distortion, he helped them to develop the skill of amnesia. Then, he directed them to a time in the future, after their problem was resolved, and asked them to hallucinate an encounter with him in this imagined future in which they told him how they resolved their difficulty. After they had described the scene to him, he had them develop amnesia for the experience and sent them on their way. Some time later they usually reported having resolved their complaints.

While Erickson's innovations are too numerous to describe in full here, we want to mention his use of indirect communication, including the use of metaphor and presupposition, and the technique of pattern intervention, which will be detailed later in the book. Erickson was one of the first therapists to recognize the impact of the therapist's communication on the assessment process. In 1965 he wrote, " . . . experience has taught me the importance of my assumption of the role of a purely passive inquirer, one who asks questions solely to receive an answer regardless of its content. An intonation of interest in the meaning of the answer is likely to induce subjects to respond as if they had

been given instructions concerning what answer to give"
(Rossi, 1980, Vol. 1, p. 94).

It must be said, however, that Erickson was not completely solution-oriented; nor was his approach always brief. He
was much too varied to be put in any one box. Nevertheless,
his work inspired much of the solution-oriented therapy we
describe.

The Mental Research Institute:
Problem-Focused Brief Therapy

In 1966, The Mental Research Institute (MRI) started a
brief therapy project. The MRI therapists were convinced
that therapy could be accomplished in a much shorter time
than the prevailing therapy standard. John Weakland, Richard Fisch, Paul Watzlawick and others worked within a deliberate time limit of 10 sessions. One organizing principle was
that they were to try to resolve the presenting problem rather than to reorganize families or develop insight. The
group's efforts to delineate specific methods for promoting
change earned them the reputation of pioneers in the psychotherapy field. Many of the principles of the MRI brief
therapy model can be considered harbingers of solution-
oriented therapy.

The treatment model is called "problem-focused" because
therapists working this way attempt to alleviate only the
specific complaints clients bring to therapy. There is no attempt to search for the underlying pathology or source of
the problem. No deliberate attempt is made to promote insight. Problems are considered to be interactional in nature.
They are viewed as being difficulties between people rather
than arising from inside individuals. People experiencing
problems are not viewed as flawed in character or as mental-
ly ill.

In this view, problems develop when ordinary life difficulties get mishandled. Once a difficulty is viewed as a "problem," the problem is maintained or made worse by people's unsuccessful attempts to solve that problem. In other words, the problem *is* the attempted solution.

For example, consider parents who are concerned about their teenage son lying to them. In all likelihood, these parents will start to scrutinize, investigate and spy on their son to determine whether he is lying to them and become quite upset when they catch him in a lie. Equally likely is the possibility that the boy will become more evasive and perhaps lie more to avoid the upsetting scenes that are becoming more and more common. Each time the parents catch him in a lie they devote more of their energies to surveillance, and he devotes more of his to clever techniques to fool them. Even when (or especially when) the parents notice that their efforts are failing to resolve the problem, they escalate these actions rather than develop a new and different plan. The boy is getting worse in their view, so more surveillance and confrontation are indicated. In the boy's view, the parents are becoming more and more restrictive and controlling, so he feels obliged to sneak and lie more to avoid their control.

This "more of the same" pattern then is the key target of therapeutic intervention within this model. Clients usually receive some variation of the suggestion that they stop trying to solve the problem in the way that they have been trying. Usually they are instructed to alter or reverse the way in which the problem has been handled heretofore, sometimes by following paradoxical directives to make the problem worse. Often this is accomplished by using the belief systems of the clients but giving them a new frame of reference within that belief system ("reframing").

For example, a family sought therapy because the father appeared "depressed." The man's wife and other family members had tried their utmost to cheer him up. When their efforts failed, they tried even harder to make him think positively. This, again, only seemed to make matters worse. The therapist told the wife that her husband did seem depressed and that his family obviously cared a great deal about him and his welfare. All the steps they had taken thus far to help him feel better were obvious signs of that love and caring. However, they were told, there might be one thing which they hadn't thought of which demonstrate their love for him even more.

The therapist then explained that he thought the father felt misunderstood, that no one could really appreciate his devastation. After all, if they really understood, how could they say "cheer up"? The therapist added, "What he really needs right now is to feel that you are really with him. You can do this by agreeing with him when he complains about things. You can also help him feel closer to you by occasionally talking about things which get you down too. This will help him feel less isolated."

Even though the actions suggested ran counter to the family's original plan, it made sense when put in this new light. Once they stopped trying to cheer him up, his "depression" lifted (Weakland, Fisch, Watzlawick, and Bodin, 1974, pp. 147–150).

The MRI theorists make the point that just as family systems can be stuck in an unsuccessful "attempted solution" pattern, so can client/therapist systems. Sometimes therapists' attempts to get clients to change can produce the opposite of the desired effect. Consequently, MRI therapists often take a pessimistic stance towards the possibility or desirability of change. If they focus on any change, they tend to warn their clients to "go slow" or to make only little changes or to watch out for relapses. Nevertheless, the MRI Brief Therapy Project showed that it was indeed possible for change to happen quite rapidly.

THE BRIEF FAMILY THERAPY CENTER:
THE TEAM THAT MADE
MILWAUKEE FAMOUS

Michele did some of her training at the Brief Family Therapy Center (BFTC) in Milwaukee, and for several years was part of the research team there. During her time there she observed the BFTC brief therapy model undergo significant shifts. There was a departure from the problem-solving, problem-focused approach from which this model emerged to an emphasis on solutions and how they worked. The team moved from a focus on identifying the patterns of interaction around the complaint in order to interrupt the problem sequence, much as in the MRI tradition, to a focus on identifying what has been working in order to identify and amplify these solution sequences (de Shazer, 1982, 1985). The model of therapy developed at BFTC is called solution-focused brief therapy.

Steve de Shazer, who has written extensively about the team's work, has used the analogy of a skeleton key to characterize this focus (1985). He contends that the therapist does not need to know a great deal about the nature of the problems brought to therapy to solve them. More relevant is the nature of solutions. It is the key that opens the door that matters most, not the nature of the lock. Analyzing and understanding the lock are unnecessary if one has a skeleton key that fits many different locks.

An interesting development from BFTC group is its declaration of the death of resistance (de Shazer, 1984). We understand the team members even held a funeral to mourn its passing. Their view is that there is no such thing as resistance (especially if you don't expect it). They assume that clients really do want to change. Admittedly, clients do not always follow therapists' suggestions, but this is not viewed as resistance. When this happens, clients are simply educat-

ing therapists as to the most productive and fitting method
of helping them change. Every client is seen as having a
unique way of cooperating and it is the task of the therapist
to identify and utilize this form of cooperation.

To this end, they developed a decision tree described below, which helped therapists identify clients' patterns of cooperating with therapeutic homework assignments. Once
the particular style of cooperation is identified, a parallel
response on the part of the therapist can be determined.
This decision tree is a variation on Erickson's "utilization
approach." At first this may seem like just a clever reframing
or relabeling of resistance, but the implications of this point
of view can be profound in therapy.

For instance, if a straightforward task is given and the
client responds by following the instructions, another
straightforward task would be indicated in later sessions to
build on the changes. In other words, this particular client is
likely to follow another straightforward suggestion.

If a client responds to a straightforward task by modifying
the task in some way, it is recommended that the therapist
use this pattern by offering easily changeable tasks, ones
with several choices or some ambiguity built into them.

If clients do not do homework tasks (either they forget or
refuse or just do not get them done), no specific homework
assignments are given. Instead, metaphors or stories of how
other people solved similar problems might be told during
the session. Clients in this group often choose one of the
solutions and employ it on their own.

If clients do the opposite of what is suggested by the
therapist, future directives will contain within them possibilities for responding in a therapeutic direction by opposing
what is suggested. For example, if a client appears to become *more* depressed between sessions after the therapist
offers change-promoting suggestions, the therapist might
tell the client instead that there are probably some good

reasons for the depression and it is essential not to change too fast.

Another milestone in the journey to becoming solution focused was when the team developed and noted the surprising effectiveness of invariant assignments and prescriptions, which they call "formula tasks." They found that several of their assignments seemed to have marked effects, regardless of the nature of the presenting complaint. That is, the same intervention might prove as effective with a bed-wetting child as with a depressed adult.

They studied one particular task, "The First Session Task," and were pleasantly surprised with the results. The task,

> Between now and the next time we meet, we (I) would like you to observe so you can describe to us (me) next time, what happens in your (pick one: family, life, marriage, relationship) that you want to continue to have happen. (de Shazer, 1985, p. 137)

was designed to focus clients' attention on the future and to create expectations of change. It reorients the person or family to noticing the good things about their situations and noticing more of the things that are going well seems to bring about even more good things.

In a follow-up survey, 50 out of 56 clients reported noticing things they wanted to continue and 46 of the 50 described at least one of these things to be something new (de Shazer et al., 1986, p. 217).

The team was intrigued with the notion that a single task could have such a uniformly positive effect in clinical situations which varied greatly. They concluded that the construction of solutions may have less to do with the specific complaints clients bring to therapy than they had previously thought. Furthermore, it became apparent after frequent use of this "First Session Task" that interventions can initiate change without the therapist's knowing much, if anything, about the problem. Formula interventions could be skeleton keys to solution.

After developing a set of skeleton key interventions (de Shazer, 1985), the BFTC team saw the implications of their success. If the solution was more important than the problem, why not focus more on the solution aspects of the situation? This led to the development of two elements of their approach, the "miracle question" and the "exception question."

The basic miracle question is: "Suppose that one night, while you were asleep, there was a miracle and this problem was solved. How would you know? What would be different?" (de Shazer, 1988, p. 5). (De Shazer has said he adapted this technique from Erickson's "pseudo-orientation in time"/ crystal ball technique described earlier and in de Shazer's *Keys to Solution in Brief Therapy*.) Contemplating this question seems to make a problem-free future more real and therefore more likely to occur. In addition, the therapist is given guidelines and concrete information to help the client go directly towards a more satisfactory future. For example, if the client says that after solving his problem he will be socializing with his friends more often, the therapist can encourage the client to go out with his friends more as part of the solution assignment.

The exception question directs the client to search in the present and the past rather than the future for solutions by focusing on those times when clients do not or have not had their problems even though they expected they would. By amplifying their descriptions of these times, clients may discover solutions that they had forgotten about or not noticed or the therapist might find clues upon which to build future solutions.

For instance, a couple who quarrel a great deal would be asked, "What is different about the times when you are getting along?" and "What does he do differently?" or "What does she do differently?" and so on. The team found that identifying and building on these exceptions was an effective way to develop solutions in many cases.

The team took the notion of focusing on the exceptions one step further. They began asking about exceptions earlier and earlier in the session. Often, after a brief description of the problem is elicited, BFTC therapists immediately ask, "So, what is different about the times when things are working?" Clients' informative responses to this question provided the team with further evidence that there is little need to know a great deal about the problem to develop solutions.

Recent developments at BFTC have included developing an "expert system" computer model that can help the team members behind the one-way mirror quickly choose solution directions based on the client's responses to questions and tasks. One of the team members, Eve Lipchik, has recently been focusing on the interviewing process as a way to shift clients' perceptions during the assessment and follow-up process. Insoo Kim Berg has been working in the areas of substance abuse and homeless families to show that these approaches can be effective with even the most difficult populations therapists have to work with.

As we mentioned earlier, we are taking a lesson from the book *In Search of Excellence* by studying the best of the best. We have extrapolated and incorporated into our work the most exciting and solution-oriented aspects of the models we describe above.

Standing on the shoulders of the giants who have preceded us, we can look into the future of psychotherapy. It is from this vantage point that solution-oriented therapy has been developed. This solution orientation challenges many typical and traditional therapy assumptions. In the next chapter we examine some of those assumptions and offer a conceptual base for solution-oriented therapy.

2.

Challenging Assumptions
Furnishing Premises for
Solution-Oriented Therapy

To contrast an explanation- and pathology-oriented approach with a solution-oriented one, we provide here an examination of the assumptions of both. Please be aware that to make our point more clearly, we have perhaps drawn the differences too starkly, and, in so doing, may have shortchanged some therapies.

COMMON ASSUMPTIONS OF MOST
CONTEMPORARY THERAPIES

Deep, Underlying Causes for Symptoms

A common assumption of many psychodynamic approaches and many family/interactional approaches is that some underlying dynamic not readily perceivable to the untrained eye is creating the problem. Problems are thus "symptoms" of some deep, underlying cause, formidable as an iceberg. Indeed, the very word "symptom" implies that what people complain about when they enter therapy is not the real problem, but always the manifestation of some underlying problem. This "iceberg" theory seems to come directly from medicine, where systemic processes give rise to specific symptoms. In medicine, treating only the symptom may be inadequate or even dangerous. This notion and this caution have been transferred to models of psychopathology and approaches to therapy.

Awareness or Insight Is Necessary for Change
or Symptom Resolution

Following the medical metaphor again, it would be unwise to treat the "symptom" without an understanding of its underlying causes. Many therapies attempt to resolve problems by providing clients with awareness of both their nature and their origin. To change anything, it is argued, one must be aware of the source or true nature of the problem.

Amelioration or Removal of Symptoms
Is Useless or Shallow at Best
and Harmful or Dangerous at Worst

Jay Haley has said, perhaps only a bit tongue-in-cheek, that he thinks that psychoanalysts avoid focusing on eliminating the symptom because they do not know how to accomplish this (personal communication, 1985). The psychoanalytic deemphasis on solutions follows from the assumption that it is not only impossible to eliminate the real problem by removing the symptom, but could also be dangerous. Temporary relief might mask the problem and reduce the client's motivation to seek treatment of "deeper" causes.

Symptoms Serve Functions

The assumption that symptoms serve functions is at the heart of even the most (seemingly) disparate current therapy approaches. Most therapists assume that symptoms occur because they serve some function or purpose in the person's life. If they did not serve a purpose, they would not persist. This idea (which, we contend, serves no purpose) persists in both individual and family therapies. The psychodynamically oriented therapist assumes that the symptom serves some intrapsychic function, while the interpersonally-oriented therapist assumes a family or interactional function. Although psychodynamically-oriented and interactionally-oriented therapists might not like to be lumped together, as we teach both groups around the world we find that they share this fundamental conviction. Following from this belief is the assumption that, if the symptom is removed without somehow taking care of the function it serves, then symptom substitution will inevitably arise. According to this belief, symptoms can redevelop in a number of ways — some other symptom will arise to take the old one's place, or the old one will come back, or someone else in the interactional field will develop a problem.

*Clients Are Ambivalent About Change
and Resistant to Therapy*

In supervising and teaching many therapists of many persuasions, we have noted a fundamental belief that clients do not really want to change or are at the least ambivalent about the possibility of change. Therefore, one has to either wait them out or get around their defenses. This position supports an adversarial model at times, with attendant military metaphors ("attacking the defenses," "being defeated by clients," "strategies to eliminate resistance," "therapist killers," etc.). One author even characterized "resistant" families as "barracudas" (Bergman, 1985). While there has been much debate about the issue in recent years (de Shazer, 1984; Stewart and Anderson, 1984), clearly the notion of resistance is not open to being disproved or proved. If you are focused on finding resistance, you will almost certainly be able to find something that looks like it.

Real Change Takes Time; Brief Interventions Are Shallow and Do Not Last

Since problems and pathology are deep-rooted or entrenched, repetitious patterns ingrained in individual or social systems, little can be expected with brief interventions and contacts other than possibly some better social or life adjustment. Even if the symptom does disappear in a brief time, it or some substitute symptom will show up sometime in the future. The client sometimes throws the therapist off the scent by having a "flight into health," i.e., by seeming to be better but really just covering up the real problem. Changes resulting from brief interventions do not last. Real change takes place the same way pathology arose—over a long period of time. Most clients and therapists seem to subscribe to the oft-repeated but unsubstantiated idea, "It will take as long to get over the problem as it took to develop it."

In relationship-oriented therapy, where the relationship between the client and the therapist is the focus of treatment, it takes quite a while to build up this relationship. In our travels we heard of a supervisor who said to one of his supervisees that he thought it took a minimum of 27 sessions to do a good assessment, to get to know a person well enough to be able to help him. While this may be an extreme case, most therapies are oriented toward long-term assessment and treatment.

Sometimes therapies that are brief and work toward clients' stated goals are said to be shallow. Jay Haley (1987, p. 25) has made the point that this convention of talking about therapies as having depth (or not) is merely a metaphor and has no scientific basis. He wonders what would have happened if, instead of "deep" and "shallow," some therapies were called "right" and some "left." Would a common dismissal of a rival's approach be to call it merely "too right" or "too left?" Suffice it to say that, if the client leaves therapy a satisfied customer and experiences no more problems clearly related to the initial one, theoretical discussions of whether therapy is deep or shallow seem superfluous.

Focus on Identifying and Correcting Pathology and Deficits

The emphasis of most therapies is on pathology and deficits. Michele presented a tape of solution-oriented therapy—a "one-shot cure"—in a workshop at a national family therapy conference. The tape showed the techniques and follow-up very clearly. After it was shown, a member of the audience commented on the rather "bubbly" mother in the family and inquired whether the therapist did not notice something very strange about her affect. She appeared to the questioner as if she were "on uppers." It seems to us that therapists often look for pathology under every possible rock. If you look for it long enough, you will surely find it.

Recently, Michele was working with a 15-year-old boy and his aunt. He had temporarily moved into her home to provide some relief for his sickly father. This boy and his father, who lived in another state, had an extremely turbulent relationship. Prior to the boy's move to his aunt's, he had been hospitalized for several months to deal with his defiant tendencies. At the end of his hospital stay, the boy was more cooperative with hospital staff, but no improvement was seen in the relationship between father and son.

At his aunt's house a great deal of improvement was observed. Though things were not perfect, he was basically cooperative, improved his school grades, sought gainful employment, and participated in family activities. Michele thought him to be a very pleasant young man who was highly motivated in treatment. His aunt was an open-minded woman who did not allow the boy's infamous reputation to dictate her expectations of him.

Several months later Michele received a call from the psychiatrist who had worked with the boy. The doctor felt the need to contact Michele to warn her about the boy's "manipulative personality." "Passive-aggressive, narcissistic and malicious" were just a few adjectives she used to describe her ex-patient. She warned Michele not to be fooled by his sweet smile. Finally, she added that she had worked with the boy's brother, who at least had the decency to "act out all over the place," while Michele's client would cleverly follow rules and appear to be cooperative, yet be deceptively calculating all the while.

Beyond Belief

Many therapists view these ideas not simply as assumptions, but as "Truths." We view them as merely beliefs; many even seem to be superstitions with precious little empirical evidence to support them. One of the problems we see with holding these ideas as unquestioned "Truths" is that the beliefs therapists hold often influence the data and outcomes in therapy. We therapists sometimes unwittingly create self-fulfilling prophecies (or perhaps we should call them other-fulfilling prophecies, in this case). If we believe that there is a deep, underlying problem, we might prompt the creation of one in the course of therapy. If we believe clients are sick and incapable, they may begin more and more to fulfill our expectations. This topic will be discussed in more detail in later chapters.

FROM PATHOLOGY TO HEALTH: THE ASSUMPTIONS OF SOLUTION-ORIENTED THERAPY

Some years ago, J. R. Burnham (1966) performed an interesting study of the effects of experimenter expectancy. He had experimenters run rats through a maze. Half the rats had portions of their brains surgically removed. The remaining half received identical incisions, but no brain tissue was removed. To outside observers, the rats looked the same. The experimenters were told that the purpose of the experiment was to learn the effects of brain lesions on learning. Some of the experimenters were told that they had brain-lesioned rats, but were actually given rats with no brain damage at all. Some of the experimenters were told that they had intact rats, but were actually given rats with the brain lesions. Some were given rats with the correct label (either lesioned or intact). The results were as follows:

1. Rats which were lesioned did not perform as well as rats which were not lesioned.
2. Rats which were thought by the experimenters to be lesioned, but which were intact, did not perform as well as rats thought to be unlesioned.
3. The lesioned rats who were thought by the experimenters to be unlesioned performed somewhat better than the unlesioned rats who were thought to be lesioned.

The second and third findings are of particular interest to us. It is clear from this and other studies (Rosenthal, 1966) that the experimenter's expectations influenced the outcome of the experiment. The actual brain state of the rat had less to do with the outcome than the experimenter's bias about the probable outcome. One can imagine the subtle difference in the ways the experimenters handled the rats and observed the data which might account for the varied performance of the rats in the maze. We are talking not about dishonesty, but about the inevitable influence of expectations on the actions and perceptions of the experimenter on the data.

Let us return to the world of therapy for a moment. Suppose you have just received a new referral along with background information such as, "Mary is incredibly resistant to therapy," or, "John is minimally brain-damaged," or, "This is a multiproblem, court-referred family." In what ways do you think that this information might influence your expectation of what is possible (or not possible) in therapy? We maintain that therapists' expectancy biases, whether positive or negative, will influence the course and outcome of therapy in a manner similar to that of the experimenter's expectancy bias in Burnham's experiment.

In her book, *Imagery in Healing*, Jeanne Achterberg (1985) offers many excellent examples of the ways in which expectations influence outcome in the medical/physical realm. She relates a story from Norman Cousins' book, *The Healing Heart* of a "critically ill patient whose cardiac muscle was irreparably compromised and for whom all therapeutic means had been exhausted. During rounds, Lown [his physician] mentioned to the staff that the patient has a 'wholesome gallop,' actually a sign of significant pathology, and usually indicative of a failing heart. Several months later the patient came for the checkup in a remarkable state of recovery. He told Dr. Lown that he knew what got him better and exactly when it occurred. ' . . . Thursday morning, when you entered with your troops, something happened that changed everything. You listened to my heart; you seemed pleased by the findings and announced to those standing about my bed that I had a "wholesome gallop."' The gentleman then went on to reason that he must have a lot of kick to his heart and therefore could not be dying. He knew instantly that he would recover" (Achterberg, 1985, p. 79, from Cousins, 1983, pp. 15–16).

Since what you expect influences what you get, solution-oriented therapists maintain those presuppositions that enhance client-therapist cooperation, empower clients, and make our work more effective and enjoyable. We hold assumptions which focus on strengths and possibilities; fortunately, these assumptions also help create self-fulfilling prophecies.

Clients Have Resources and Strengths to Resolve Complaints

Erickson's work with "Ma" (related in our Introduction) points to the idea that each person already has skills and resources which can be used to resolve complaints. It is the task of the therapist to access these abilities and put them to use. Frequently, clients overwhelmed by life's difficulties lose sight of their problem-solving strengths. They may simply need to be reminded of the tools with which they are equipped to develop long-lasting, satisfying solutions. At other times, they may have some capabilities that can be added to or honed in order to help them sort out their situations.

A first grade teacher came to Michele for treatment because she could no longer deal with her frustrating relationship with her 15-year-old daughter; she was at her wit's end. She explained that constant coaxing, reminding, heart-to-heart talks, and screaming matches did not make her daugh-

ter more cooperative at home. *According to her mother, the girl was self-indulgent, defiant, and disrespectful.*

It became evident that the single method this woman used to handle her daughter was that of verbalizing her displeasure. Though she would occasionally vary her volume, she never considered any other form of discipline. Mother believed that her daughter should have more concern for her feelings and comply for that reason. Unfortunately her daughter didn't agree.

All that was necessary to help this woman get unstuck was to remind her of her work with first graders. "All teachers know that children have different learning styles," we reminded her. "Some are visual learners and some are auditory learners." She joined in the conversation by offering additional information regarding her students' preferred learning styles. "The teaching method must match the learning style of the individual student for learning to occur." She heartily agreed. We suggested that she mistakenly took her daughter to be an auditory learner and needed to reevaluate the girl's real approach to learning. Having accessed her abundant skills, she had no difficulty becoming more creative and effective in her responses to her daughter.

Change Is Constant

If you assume change is constant, you will behave as if change were inevitable. Through verbal and nonverbal means clients will be given the impression that it would be surprising if the presenting complaint were to persist. Physicists tell us that all is flux; atoms and molecules are constantly moving and rearranging themselves in the physical universe. Biologists tell us that we create new cells in our bodies constantly, so that eventually we have an almost totally new set of cells in our bodies. We see the universe as one of change. In fact, we think that people's situations are changing all the time. Their *views* of the situations are what re-main the same when they report that nothing has changed.

A mother and teenage daughter seen at Michele's agency were asked to report the results of the homework assignment they had been given during the first session. The task was designed to reduce the number of arguments between them, since the mother had previously complained that they argued constantly. The daughter began describing in great detail an argument that had occurred during the week. Mother added her impressions of the altercation. Ten min-utes into this discussion, the therapist interrupted them by asking, "By the way, how was the rest of the week?" Mother's demeanor changed abruptly. "Oh," she said, "She was a per-fect angel!! Aside from that one argument she was great."

It is our guess that, if the therapist had allowed this pair to discuss their fight, they could and would have done so for most of the session. Furthermore, it is likely that they would have left the session focused on the difficulties in their rela-tionship, even though the vast majority of the week went exceedingly well. In all probability this would have had detri-mental effects on their relationship. Fortunately for these clients, the therapist's assumption that "change is inevitable" leads her to devote the remainder of the session to exploring what contributed to their having a relatively peaceful week.

Similarly, how often does it happen that, though a hus-band and wife have had an extremely amicable week or two, a disagreement they had on the way to the therapist's office leads the therapist to believe that no improvement has taken place? The therapist sees two angry individuals and makes instantaneous, sometimes unconscious, assumptions about their progress, thereby becoming discouraged. As the spouses eagerly explain the nature of their disagreement (thinking that that is what they are in therapy for), they sense the therapist's growing discouragement and memories of the good times from the week fade.

Conversely, when we assure clients that their fight will be discussed after checking on the homework (offering them an opportunity to report on the week's positive events), the positive feelings arising from this discussion create quite a different context in which to later rehash the disagreement, if this is even necessary at that point. Memories of disagreement can also be dulled in this manner. It is obvious that therapists can do a great deal to influence clients' perceptions regarding the inevitability of change and what is "supposed" to happen during the therapy session.

As our initial discussion indicated, we think that the therapist channels the discussion in the session in a certain direction, based on biases and assumptions. Since the solution-oriented therapist is focused on the pervasiveness of change, she shifts the focus of the conversation away from how things have stayed the same and toward how things have changed.

The Therapist's Job Is to Identify and Amplify Change

> As therapists, clearly we have a duty. First, to achieve clarity in ourselves; and then to look for every sign of clarity in others and to implement them and reinforce them in whatever is sane in them.
>
> — Gregory Bateson (1972, p. 487)

It should be clear from the examples above that as therapists we help to create a particular reality by the questions we ask and the topics we choose to focus upon, as well as those we choose to ignore. In the smorgasbord of information supplied to us by our clients, we think it important to focus on what seems to be working, however small, to label it as worthwhile, and to work toward amplifying it. In describing his observations of Erickson's work, Haley wrote, "It is also characteristic of Erickson's family work that he seeks a small change and enlarges upon it. If the change is in a crucial area, what appears small can change the whole system. Sometimes he uses the analogy of a hole in a dam; it does not take a very large hole to lead to a change in the structure of the whole dam" (1973, pp. 34–35).

It Is Usually Unnecessary to Know a Great Deal about the Complaint in Order to Resolve It

Typically, solution-oriented therapists do not find it useful to gather extensive historical information about the presenting problem. Sometimes only a bare minimum of information is necessary to begin resolving the complaint. We have found that therapists often get stuck because they have too much information rather than too little, or too much information about the problem and too little about the solution.

Several years ago Michele saw a mother and her 15-year-old daughter in therapy. At the start of the first session, she asked a question about what positive changes the two had noticed in the situation prior to the session. The mother reported about 15 minutes' worth of positive material on all the changes she had observed between calling for the appointment and keeping the appointment. She said, "I am more relaxed because my daughter seems happier and more relaxed. . . . I can concentrate at work much better. . . . I've realized my own role in keeping this going and I have made some changes. . . . Her father seems to be off her back, so I'm feeling much better." Then the girl added her own account of improvements, which included being more relaxed; getting along better with her friends, being able to concen-

trate at school, and being relieved that her mother felt better.

Halfway through these reports of change (which sounded like what is said during a final session of successful treatment), Michele realized that she knew nothing about the complaint at all. As the clients continued to list changes, she wondered what to do next, since she was overwhelmed by the number and magnitude of the reported changes. She considered simply asking, "So what needs to happen for both of you to continue these changes?" but at that time it was counter-intuitive to consider solving a problem about which one knew nothing.

Instead she resorted to, "So what can I help you with?" It was evident as soon as she asked this question that she had reversed the forward momentum initiated by her earlier question. Both mother and daughter complied by offering their accounts of the difficulties they were experiencing. Inadvertently, Michele had distracted them from the change process.

Rather than detailed information about the complaint, what appears to be significant for solution-oriented therapists is what clients are already doing that is working. When clients identify times when the problem bringing them to treatment is not troublesome, there is much to be learned from these exceptions. Whatever is different about these trouble-free times can be identified, and the client can learn to do what's working again and again, thereby "crowding out" the problem. It is as if there is a television screen that gets filled with whatever is in front of the camera of therapeutic conversation. If the camera is focused mainly on problems and pathology, both therapists and clients perceive problems and pathology. If the focus of inquiry and discussion is on solutions and abilities, those images dominate the screen. In a similar manner, if clients can be brought to either perceive or act upon strengths and solutions outside of the session, that perception or experience will fill the screen of their lives outside of therapy as well.

It Is Not Necessary to Know the Cause or Function of a Complaint to Resolve It

Solution-oriented therapists do not accept the belief that symptoms (what we will call "complaints") serve functions for individuals, relationships or families. Even the most perceptive and creative hypotheses about the possible function of a symptom will not offer therapists a clue about how people can change. It simply suggests how people's lives have become static and why they remain that way.

> Essentially, the idea that symptoms serve functions has its roots in psychoanalytic theory. The doctrine of symptom substitution held that psychological problems represented underlying conflicts and any focus on symptom removal rather than the underlying issue, would, at best, merely lead to the appearance of yet another symptom. . . .
>
> It has never been empirically demonstrated that elimination of symptoms must inevitably lead to family disruption or new symptoms in other family members. It certainly was not the case in the 300 or so case records that I examined at MRI [Mental Research Institute]. The most typical reaction of families to the improvement of a member is relief. . . .
>
> Nevertheless, a therapist who believes that symptoms serve functions may actually encourage family disruption. When therapy is guided by the belief in the function of symptoms, true collaboration with families becomes difficult. . . . The most serious problem with the function-of-symptoms notion is that it can become an anti-therapeutic, self-fulfilling prophecy. (Coyne, 1985, pp. 60–61)

Prior to beginning treatment, most clients have speculated (ad nauseam) about the causes and reasons for their difficulties. Seldom does this type of analysis move them toward solution; if it did, they would not be seeking treatment. Knowing "why" one overeats rarely helps to curb appetites or change eating habits.

Due to prior therapy experiences, to images the media has provided about the therapy process, or to a cultural belief in the validity of a search for causes, many clients tell us that their goal for treatment is to understand "why" they are having their particular problem. To this we respond, "Would it be enough if the problem were to disappear and you never understood why you had it?" Generally, clients agree that alleviation of the complaint is what they are really after. They just thought they had to understand the problem before they resolved it.

A Small Change Is All That Is Necessary; A Change in One Part of the System Can Affect Change in Another Part of the System

People in a rut often talk about vicious circles. They know it might help their depression to get out and do something, but they're too depressed to get out and do something. Recognizing their inability to take action, they get even more depressed, which makes them feel even less like getting out, and so on.

This tendency for thoughts and actions to escalate can also work in the opposite direction. Once a small positive change is made, people feel optimistic and a bit more confident about tackling further changes. Couples seeking treatment often provide clear examples of this phenomenon. Blaming and withholding typically characterize these relationships. However, when person A undertakes one small gesture which pleases person B, person B reciprocates, which in turn stimulates person A to respond in kind, and so on. (Perhaps this could be called a "benevolent spiral.")

Erickson used the metaphor of a snowball rolling down a mountain to describe the importance of small changes. The snowball metaphor says that once the ball gets rolling, the therapist merely needs to stay out of the way. This is in contrast to the "Sisyphus" model of therapy, (after the Greek myth of Sisyphus) in which the therapist helps the client or the family roll the rock of the problem up to the top of the mountain only to discover that at the beginning of the next session the rock is again at the bottom of the mountain. Some therapists even roll the rock up to the top of the mountain while the family watches from below.

Another aspect of change is that it is contagious; a change in one part of the system effects change in another part of the system. At workshops we sometimes show a videotape of a mother and son who are complaining about many things, including Grandma (who is not present in the session) and her interfering behavior. The comment most frequently made by observers after seeing the first session is that the therapist must include Grandma in session two in order to work out their differences. Session two begins with mother reporting that things are greatly improved and her son wholeheartedly agreeing. She adds that Grandma minded her own business this week, which pleases them. This leaves workshop participants puzzled, however, because the therapist gave no homework task or messages relating to Grandma. What then could account for this sudden change in her annoying behavior?

We have repeatedly observed that a change in one part of the family leads to changes in other parts of the family. Likewise, a small change in one part of an individual's life often creates a ripple effect in other areas. Envision the movement of a mobile. Shortly after one small piece has been set in motion, the entire mobile is turning, rotating and revolving. Since change appears to yield more change, solution-oriented therapists, instead of worrying about symptom substitution or relapse at the end of therapy, envision a future which is even brighter than the client's situation at termination. We have the sense that the positive changes will at least continue and may expand and have beneficial effects in other areas of the person's life.

Indeed, according to follow-up studies performed at the Brief Family Therapy Center and the Mental Research Institute, there appears to be some empirical basis for this optimism. One of the several follow-up questions used is, "Have any old problems that were not directly dealt with in therapy improved since you finished therapy at BFTC?" In one particular study, 15 out of 23 clients surveyed reported improvement in other areas (de Shazer, 1985, pp. 156–157). A follow-up study done at the McHenry County (Illinois) Youth Service Bureau, where Michele works, using the same questions, yielded approximately the same results, with 67% of clients surveyed reporting improvements in other areas.

Clients Define the Goal

In the videotaped example above, mother tells the therapist that her goal for therapy is to be less sarcastic with her son and to fight less with him. However, when we ask therapists who view the tape what they think the goals should be, they suggest such things as, "Mother [who is single] needs a boyfriend," "Mother needs to learn to let go of her son," "They need to have more eye contact," and "They need to move out of Grandma's house." All of these suggestions may be good ones, but they have little to do with the goals the client has set for herself. Sometimes when we do this exercise, therapists cannot even recall the mother's stated goals.

Solution-oriented therapists don't believe that there is any single "correct" or "valid" way to live one's life. We have come to understand that what is unacceptable behavior in one family or for one person is desirable behavior in another. Therefore, clients, not therapists, identify the goals to be accomplished in treatment. (This is different from identifying problems, which we view as a co-creation between clients and therapists.)

Therapists are trained to see pathology, so in the situation above they might be certain that it is pathological for the mother and son to live with the Grandma. We think that decision is best left to the people involved (Grandma, mother and son), and we can work towards their stated goals without imposing upon them our ideas about how they should live after treatment is successful.

Erickson has said in this regard, "Each person is a unique individual. Hence, psychotherapy should be formulated to meet the uniqueness of the individual's needs, rather than tailoring the person to fit the Procrustean bed of a hypothetical theory of human behavior" (Zeig, 1982, p. vii).

One final thought about goal-setting in therapy. We have worked with many clients whose earlier therapy experiences have been disappointing for the following reason: Contrary to what the client identified as the goal, the therapist insisted that he or she knew what the real problem was, and therefore, what the treatment goal should be. Frequently, these clients say, "We brought our son in for some counseling for his behavior problem but the therapist said we are really having marital problems and should be working on the marriage instead. We were angry and decided not to go back."

Since we do not believe that there is such a thing as "the real problem" underlying the complaint, nor do we believe that therapists are better equipped to decide how their clients should live their lives, we ask our people seeking our help to establish their own goals for treatment. Only in rare circumstances do we make alternate suggestions to our clients' goals. The establishment of illegal goals, such as child abuse, is one obvious exception. The handling of patently unattainable or unrealistic goals is another exception which is dealt with more fully in later sections.

In most other cases, clients set their own goals. If the couple in the above situation want to work on their son's behavior, that's exactly what we will do. Needless to say, it is predictable for the couple to get along better when they do not have to argue about their son's misbehavior. There is more than one way to skin a cat.

Rapid Change or Resolution of Problems Is Possible

We believe that, as a result of our interaction during the first session, our clients will gain a new, more productive, and optimistic view of their situations. If, after the first session, they still think their situation needs improvement, we fully expect them to go home and do what is necessary to make their lives more satisfying. It is therefore common for significant changes to be reported during session two and for these changes to be quite durable. Average length of treatment for therapists working this way varies, but is generally under ten sessions, usually more like four or five, and occasionally only one.

The concerns clients bring to solution-oriented therapists do not differ from those of clients seeking other types of treatment. Yet rapid resolution of problems or "spontaneous healing" is not commonly reported within other treatment modalities. Again, we are convinced that therapists and clients co-create realities. The therapist's belief about what can ultimately be achieved may be the most significant factor contributing to clients' expectations of change.

Another intriguing illustration of rapid healing is portrayed in *Imagery in Healing* (Achterberg, 1985, pp. 82–83). A medical writer with a specialization in cancer was diagnosed as having a brain tumor and given six months to live. However, when she reviewed the national cancer statistics with someone who helped her interpret them, she discovered that, while it is true that the average or median life expectancy was six months, 38% of all patients in her age group could be expected to live for three years, and 27% would live at least ten years and be proclaimed cured after that length of time. When she learned about the new statistics, she thought, "I've got it made." Following this, " . . . she began thinking and acting like a healthy person again. Within two days her speech cleared, her memory improved, and a persistent cough disappeared. She insisted on a program of physical therapy to help strengthen her weak arm and hand, and requested that her high doses of tranquilizers and sleeping pills be reduced. The neurologist working in consultation with us was astounded at her rapid progress."

There Is No One "Right" Way to View Things;
Different Views May Be Just as Valid and
May Fit the Facts Just as Well

In the classic Japanese movie, Rashomon, the story of a murder is told through the eyes and memories of several different observers. What is so intriguing about this story is that, though the storytellers describe the same events, their descriptions differ tremendously. There is no way to ascertain which of the views is most "correct"; rather, it is evident that each view is merely a small portion of the total picture and is colored by each person's biases and assumptions.

When we work with couples and families in therapy, we are reminded of the Rashomon effect. Sometimes when two people describe an event, an argument, or even the story line in a movie, it is hard to believe they both observed the same thing. As the different views are described, rather than thinking of each as "right" or "wrong," we assume that each person's perception represents an equally valid, integral part of the situation.

While we do not think that there are any correct or incorrect points of view, we do believe that there are more or less useful viewpoints. That is, the views that people hold about their problems enhance or diminish the likelihood of solution. Useful views offer an escape from the psychological webs people weave. Views that keep them stuck are simply not useful.

For example, although no one might disagree with the "facts" of the situation, "Steve has been cutting school and is failing five classes," there may be hearty disagreement about the "meaning" of this behavior. Steve's behavior might be described as spiteful and lazy. Dad may say that his cutting school is simply a rebellious, belligerent act. Or perhaps Steve's parents may conjecture that he is having a problem with his self-esteem since his move to the new school six months ago. Mom might add that they have been under a great deal of stress lately due to financial problems and that Steve is probably reflecting the tension at home. A third view might be that Steve's missing school is but one example of his erratic behavior in general, which is symptomatic of his sugar allergy.

These views will influence how one goes about the business of trying to reduce Steve's truant behavior. Having deemed Steve to be belligerent and lazy, his parents will, in all likelihood, use punishment or discipline to force him to improve his attendance. If Steve is thought to have a self-esteem problem, however, lenthy "heart-to-hearts" and discussions ("What's wrong? Tell me what's really upsetting you") are the rule. Therapy appointments are often scheduled to "get at the root of the problem." Parents with this point of view generally do not consider using negative consequences (punishments) for undesirable behavior. Likewise, if the parents are convinced that the cause of their child's behavior is physiological, then of course a biochemical treatment is indicated and other approaches will not be sought or welcomed.

So, the meanings people attribute to behavior limit the range of alternatives they will use to deal with a situation. If the methods used do not produce a satisfactory outcome, the original assumption about the meaning of the behavior is generally not questioned. If it were, new meanings might be considered, which in turn might prompt a different, perhaps more effective, approach. Instead, people often redouble their efforts to solve the problem in an ineffective way, thinking that by doing it more, harder, or better (e.g., more punishments, more heart-to-hearts, and so on) they will finally solve it (the MRI group's "more of the same"; Watzlawick, Weakland, and Fisch, 1974). In their persistence they are reminiscent of "tourists traveling in non-English speaking countries who, when their requests are not understood by the natives, repeat their requests louder" (Weiner-Davis, 1984, p. 47).

Sometimes all that is necessary to initiate significant change is a shift in the person's perception of the situation. For example, a mother was terribly concerned about her teenage daughter. She reported that the girl seemed depressed because she spent a great deal of time alone in her room, and when she did join the family for meals, she was often quiet and appeared eager to return to her room when she was done eating. As is often the case in these situations, Mom had tried to help by asking her daughter, "Are you okay? What's wrong? Are you depressed?" To avoid such questioning the girl retreated even further.

We asked Mom how she was able to tell the difference between "depression" and "normal teenage moodiness." She reflected a moment on our question and said she had not really considered the possibility that her daughter was simply moody. This new view of the old situation greatly relieved her. The next time she observed her daughter quietly reading in her room, she thought nothing of it and settled down on the couch to read a good book herself. The girl noticed something was different when her mother wasn't standing in her doorway checking up on her; being curious about this, she walked downstairs to see what was going on. The girl's presence downstairs reinforced mother's new perception of her daughter as healthy, and so on.

*Focus Is on What Is Possible and Changeable,
Rather Than What Is Impossible
and Intractable*

As change-oriented therapists, we want to focus our attention on the changing and changeable aspects of our clients' experiences. We do not, therefore, focus on entities or aspects of the client or the client's situation that are not amenable to change.

One of the current fads in therapy is the diagnosis of "borderline personality." We have been taking surveys in our workshops and have yet to find someone who has cured or changed a borderline personality. The best one can do with that diagnosis, short of years of intensive and potentially unsuccessful therapy, is to manage the disorder.

Perhaps this is the crux of the disagreement between solution-oriented therapists and long-term therapists of other orientations. Those of us who are more solution-oriented like to work with fairly well defined goals that are realizable within a reasonable amount of time (that is, well short of Alby Singer's 20 years). Long-term therapists often contract, wittingly or unwittingly, to try to change people's relatively fixed characteristics, like their personalities and their complexes. To cure a borderline personality is beyond our ken, but to help a person get a job or make friends or have a satisfying sexual relationship or refrain from cutting herself is well within our abilities.

We therefore focus on those aspects of the person's situation that seem most changeable, knowing that to start positive changes and to help the person realize small goals may have wider and unexpected effects in other areas (perhaps even in his "personality"). We avoid psychological constructs not useful for change. Personality constructs can help us make sense of the complexity of the people, but a whole new set of constructs is needed to help people change.

Jay Haley (1976) has made this point well:

> To label a child as "delinquent" or as suffering from "minimal brain dysfunction," or to label an adult as an "alcoholic" or a "schizophrenic," means that one is participating in the creation of a problem in such a way that change is made more difficult. A therapist who describes a family situation as characterized by "a dominating mother and a passive father," or "a symbiotic relationship between mother and daughter," has created problems, although the therapist might think he is merely identifying the problems put before him. The way in which one labels a human dilemma can crystallize a problem and make it chronic.

3.

The Uncertainty Principle in Therapy
Co-creating Solvable Problems

> If therapy is to end properly, it must begin properly —
> by negotiating a solvable problem. . . . The act of thera-
> py begins with the way the problem is examined.
>
> —Jay Haley, *Problem Solving Therapy*, p. 9

Iatrogenic disease is the name given to those medical problems that are caused or made worse by the approach taken
by the doctor who is treating the problem. Tardive dyskine-
sia, a Parkinsonian-like disease caused by long-term use of
psychiatric drugs (neuroleptics), is an example. Here we
want to focus on techniques of iatrogenic health, that is,
health that is promoted or created by the therapeutic interaction. In 1961, while giving a lecture, Erickson, always
ahead of his time, spoke on this subject. "While I have read a
number of articles on this subject of iatrogenic disease, and
have heard many discussions about it, there is one topic on
which I haven't seen much written about and that is iatrogenic health. Iatrogenic health is a most important consideration — much more important than iatrogenic disease" (Rossi
and Ryan, 1986, p. 140). In echoing his sentiment, we want
to introduce you to the use of techniques that can create a

"placebo effect" in the direction of solution and healing rather than inadvertently in the direction of problems and
pathology.

CO-CREATING REALITIES

In our view it is a mistake to think about the interviewing
process in the same way that one would think about a medical doctor's collecting information about a physical symptom. The doctor wants to know the facts about the broken
bone. He wants data about the events which took place
outside his office. Therefore, he asks: "How did this happen?" "How long ago did you fall?" "Where does it hurt?" "Is
the swelling more or less than before?" His ability to gather
accurate information about the symptom will help him
make an appropriate diagnosis, which will indicate the correct treatment plan. Therapy is different. The complaints
clients bring to treatment are not like broken bones or sore
throats. As therapists we strongly influence clients' perceptions and experience of their situations during the interview
process. What we choose to focus upon, what we choose to
ignore, the way in which we word our questions, whether we
decide to interrupt or remain silent—all help shape the picture of the client's situation.

For example, when a person says, "I am totally out of
control of my life," there are many directions a therapist
might pursue. Remaining silent and allowing the client to
elaborate is one of many possibilities. Choices about which
question(s) to ask are far from simple. One could ask for a
more detailed account of the perception of being out of
control—in other words, what are the symptoms, how long
have they existed and so on. This question reifies the problem as a serious one.

Another choice of questions might be, "What gives you
the impression that things seem difficult to handle?" This

question is designed to introduce some uncertainty into the problem definition. A third possibility is, "What is different about the days when things seem manageable?" This question implies that there are days when the problem is nonexistent and explores what is different about them.

It is apparent that each of the three questions will lead the therapist and client into a completely different realm of discourse. Obviously, therapist-client interactions can greatly influence the client's perceptions.

Another useful way of thinking about this perception-shaping process is illustrated by the following analogy. The scene is the courtroom. The defense attorney stands, his client is sworn in. The attorney proceeds with a line of inquiry which is designed to elicit certain "factual" information about his client. Undoubtedly, the "facts" upon which the defense attorney focuses will present his client in the most positive light possible. He hopes that, at the end of his testimony, the client will be seen as innocent of the crimes of which he has been accused, a fine upstanding individual in his community, a good father, loyal husband, and a man of high moral standards.

Enter the prosecuting attorney. Though he too asks "factual" questions, they are undoubtedly chosen to elicit information harmful to the man's case. A completely different picture of the man's character will emerge, suggesting that the jury rule out the possibility that he is innocent.

We consider ourselves "defense therapists." The questions we ask elicit information about strengths, abilities, and resources. Perceptions of problems often change significantly in the context of this sort of questioning. We are participants in the co-creation of our clients' reality. Clients who step into our offices have unwittingly entered "The Twilight Zone," embarking on a mind-altering experience.

Prior to our becoming solution-oriented therapists, we both used several different models and therapy approaches.

We have noticed that not only are different results achieved with different models and approaches, but different data also emerge during the assessment process, leading to different definitions of the problem. In other words, problem definition in therapy is a function of the assessment process. The assessment process is influenced by the therapist's metaphors and assumptions with regard to people and the nature of problems and by the theory of resolution he or she holds. (We have never had a client with an unresolved oedipal conflict or an overactive superego. Just lucky, we suppose!) It is a bit like the Heisenberg uncertainty principle in physics—the way that one observes alters the data being observed.

Bill makes spritz cookies every year at Christmas—it's a family tradition. He uses a cookie press to make these cookies. If you've never seen a cookie press, we'll explain it to you. Once the dough is made up, it is put into a tubular device with a mold on the end. The dough is forced through the mold at the end so that it comes out looking like a camel or, if the mold is changed, like a Christmas tree or a Santa Claus. The dough is the same, but the shape changes. The cookies are then cooked and harden into that mold's shape.

The raw data of the client's (or clients') complaint are like Bill's cookie dough. It is shaped by the therapeutic interaction during and after assessment into a more solid "presenting problem." If the client walks into a behaviorist's office, he or she will leave with a behavioral problem. If clients choose psychoanalysts' offices, they will leave with unresolved issues from childhood as the focus of the problem. If a client seeks help from a Jungian analyst, he or she is likely to get a problem that can be treated most effectively by examining symbolism in the client's dreams.

It is not that therapists randomly assign problems to clients. The problems are derived from the raw data of the clients' complaints. They are, in our view, interpersonally negotiated, or co-created. It is uncanny, though, how similar the problems of clients seeing a therapist with a particular perspective will look and how different they will look from those of clients seeing a therapist from a different school.

The implications of this point are exciting. If problems are negotiable, one might as well negotiate a problem that is possible—even easy—to solve. Usually clients have already come up with some sort of problem definition that has not sorted out the situation. We prefer to negotiate a problem definition that is within the power of both the client and the therapist to solve. We usually offer new, more workable problem definitions and/or listen for a hint of something in the client's complaint that can be solved. One could think of it as dancing. There is a constant interchange during the dance so that after a while it is hard to tell who is leading and who is following. Every dancer has a style; the blending of the two styles together is what makes the dance. Our style is to dance to the rhythms of strengths, solutions, and competence. Our clients often follow our lead and begin to contribute their own piece to that dance.

Beware of Reifying the Client's Reality: All Is Process

One of the contributions of interactional approaches to therapy has been the notion that people's experience is greatly influenced by the contexts in which they live. Anthropologists have made similar observations. "Reality" is not a fixed, static given. It is influenced by our cultures and the interactions we have with one another. It is influenced by the language we speak, the words we use, the world views we share that are reflected in those words. It is with this in mind that we stress that therapy is like a little culture or society created in the session. This culture will, in our view, greatly influence clients' feelings, thoughts, reports, and perceptions.

Consider the situation when a small child falls down and skins his knee. He often looks around at his parents or other people to get a clue as to how he should treat this incident. Is it something to be upset about? If he sees or hears great concern or upset from those around, he will usually start to cry. If he is picked up, brushed off, given a pat on the bottom, and sent on his way, he will usually go off without so much as a whimper. Children, especially young ones, look for cues from their contexts to help them determine what to feel or think about a situation.

We view the therapy situation in much the same way. If a therapist gives a client verbal and/or nonverbal messages that the point of this encounter is for the client to experience and express some intense emotion, such as crying or an angry outburst, very likely that will happen in the course of the session. We think that people often do not know what they feel about situations and are very influenced by contextual cues. Instead of searching, therefore, for the real underlying feelings, problems, or views of clients, we prefer to actively influence and co-create those experiences.

Indeed, we think that all therapists do this regardless of their view on the matter. So it may come as no surprise that we believe that there is no such thing as the "real problem" in therapy. We do not try to determine some a priori position that the client might hold about his or her problem, as some therapies do (e.g., the MRI brief therapists), because we do not believe that such a "position" exists as a fixed entity. We do not search for the client's "real" feelings, thoughts, or other such fixed, static psychological/emotional entities.

DIRECTIONS FOR NEGOTIATION

Dissolve the Idea That There Is a Problem

THERAPIST   What can I help you with?
CLIENT   (Flat affect) Hm. Who knows? I went into a massive

depression and so I decided maybe I needed to talk to somebody that didn't know me that could give me maybe, or maybe just talking it out would clear my head. I don't know. Um. My job is getting sickening. I'm on the verge of smacking my roommate. Last week got kind of rough with my roommate and—we've gotten along for a long time. I guess I just finally let it get to me and finally was sick of it. And ah, so I don't know, last week's been a, with work, inventory and her, just, I don't know, I think I need to get out of here, is what I need to do.

THERAPIST   Need to get out of where?

CLIENT   Wisconsin, maybe. I don't know, maybe start . . . maybe do something different with my life.

[Twenty minutes into the interview]

CLIENT   (Smiling) I know, it sounds like I really don't need to talk to anybody, doesn't it? I have been doing really well . . .

How is it possible that this client could have expressed two such vastly different perceptions of her life situation within such a short period of time? Solution-oriented therapists are familiar with this dramatic turnabout in their sessions; there is nothing unusual or peculiar about this. Clients frequently leave the first session with a completely new outlook on their lives.

We begin each first session with the assumption that it is possible to negotiate a therapeutic reality that dissolves the idea that there is a "problem." Using a variety of techniques described in the following chapter, we are able to help people see their situations in new ways. Sometimes our clients at the end of the first session tell us things like, "I guess things aren't as bad as I thought," or "I'm not really sure why I came here today," or "I don't think I need to schedule another appointment if I just keep doing what I have been doing." When we do workshops we facetiously tell therapists that if they learn how to dissolve the idea that there is a problem, they won't need to know how to do therapy.

Negotiate a Solvable Problem

If, during the course of our initial discussion, we are not successful in eliminating the problem, our next priority is to make the problem appear more manageable and less impervious to creative problem-solving. Reducing the size of the problem in the client's eyes by making it appear more manageable is our goal. The usual way we do this is to get specific and, of course, to ask about times when the client does not experience the problem.

A client sought Bill's help for depression. He initially stated that he was depressed "all the time" and that he was concerned that it had started to affect his work. When the questioning got more specific, it turned out that he experienced severe depression only on the weekends. More specific questioning revealed that it was almost always Sunday afternoons that were the focus of the depression. Other times he might become a bit depressed, but because he was busy at work and with friends, he rarely had time to sink deeply into depression. With this new perception of the severity and length of the problem, it became a much more manageable goal to work on alternative plans for Sunday afternoons.

Frame Towards the Idea That Clients Have All the Abilities and Resources to Solve the Problem

An equally important goal is to create a context in which our clients feel better equipped to resolve their difficulties than when they walked into our office. We have noticed that when people are experiencing difficulties, they often forget that they have resources and strengths. Perhaps this is a matter of developing tunnel vision. Sometimes clients do not make a connection between skills and abilities they have in an apparently unrelated area that can help them resolve their problems. It is our job to create an atmosphere that facilitates the realization of strengths and abilities. The following chapter will explain how we accomplish this.

4.

Watch Your Language
Having a Conversation for Change

We have already discussed the notion that different therapeutic realities are created in different therapists' offices. Here we examine one part of that creation of a therapeutic reality: language. Language has a way of reifying, solidifying certain views of reality. It can also be used as a tool to question unhelpful certainties. So we have learned to be very careful about the ways we use language in therapy.

Ericksonian hypnotists who observe the sessions in which we use no formal hypnosis comment on the way in which we use language to create an expectancy of change just as they do when using hypnosis. We agree and believe furthermore that the creative and mindful use of language is perhaps the single most influential indirect method for creating contexts in which change is perceived to be inevitable.

Other than matching clients' language, a strategy described below which is primarily a joining technique, the other methods discussed are geared toward affecting changes in perception and behavior. What these other methods have in common is their use of presuppositions. Presuppositions are ways of talking that presume something without stating it directly. Perhaps you know the infamous courtroom question, "Have you stopped beating your wife?" If the witness were instructed to answer the question yes or no, he would be forced into accepting the presupposition that he had beaten his wife.

In a similar manner, therapists can use presuppositions to introduce change notions and expectations in the therapy session. If a therapist asks, "What will be different in your life when therapy is successful?", he or she is not merely seeking information but also implicitly introducing the idea that therapy will be successful. Similarly, when one opens the therapy session with the question, "What problem can I help you with?" or "What do you see as the problem?", it is presumed that there is a problem and, in the former question, one which requires an expert's assistance. On the other hand, "What brings you here?" does not presume the existence of a problem.

Just as one cannot "not communicate" (Watzlawick, Weakland, and Fisch, 1974), for even silence speaks loudly, it is equally impossible to speak without revealing the presuppositions we hold about the world. As therapists, we continually give our clients clues, both subtle and obvious, as to our views of them and their prospects for change. We think, therefore, that it is imperative to be aware of these communications in therapy and to use them to facilitate the change process.

MATCHING THE CLIENT'S LANGUAGE

A tried and true principle from the work of Milton Erickson and others is: *Initially use the words that clients use as a means of joining with them and building rapport.*

People select particular words to reflect their experiences. The words chosen carry with them certain connotations for the speaker. To the extent that as therapists we match our clients' language, clients typically come to believe that we understand, appreciate, and identify with their subjective experiences. Rapport and cooperation are built upon this belief. Clients often visibly relax when they sense that they are understood.

Erickson describes a fascinating case in which he went to extremes to speak the client's language. His efforts had important implications for change.

Erickson worked with a man the hospital staff called George (because no one had been able to communicate with him to find out his name) who had been hospitalized for five years before Erickson treated him. He had been found wandering around talking in nonsense syllables or "word salad." Erickson had a secretary sit at a desk near where George sat where, on a daily basis, he unsuccessfully tried to communicate with passersby. She was to transcribe his words. When Erickson studied the transcripts, he could find no meaningful communications hidden in them, so he decided to learn to speak this man's word salad and use that as a way to open up the communication lines. Erickson introduced himself to George and was immediately greeted with a few derisive sentences of word salad. When Erickson responded in kind with a friendly few sentences of word salad, the man was initially skeptical, but soon warmed to Erickson when he found Erickson speaking his language. Day after day, they carried on their word salad conversations, always in the most meaningful tones. Gradually, George began to intersperse a few recognizable words within the nonsense. Erickson asked him what his name was. "O'Donovan," replied the man, "and it's about time somebody who can talk sense asked me!" Each day, more and more of their conversations were carried on in recognizable English, until George rarely spoke in nonsense syllables. He was released from the hospital and seemed to adjust well to life following his release. (Rossi, 1980, Vol. 4, pp. 213–215)

Learning the Hard Way

While most of us do not have the persistence (or time) that Erickson had in working with some of his clients, there are a few simple things which can be done to benefit from the lessons Erickson taught. Consider the following example of how *not* to join with clients:

Some years ago Michele was seeing a couple for marital therapy. The wife described a "disagreement" which took place between her and her husband one evening. Raised voices and harsh words were exchanged before her husband finally left the room. Later in the session Michele referred back to that evening saying, "Remember that fight you had the other night?" The woman corrected her, stating, "We didn't fight; we had a disagreement." In reminding the woman that there were raised voices and an abrupt ending to the interaction, Michele argued that it was indeed "a fight." To this the woman replied, "Absolutely not, we were simply discussing." Before Michele and her client knew it, they were arguing about whether it was a fight or a discussion.

In retrospect there is something humorous about this story, yet there were serious therapeutic ramifications at the time. The client believed that Michele did not understand or appreciate her subjective experience. She distanced herself at that juncture in the session; shortly after this session the couple dropped out of treatment. Although it is unlikely that Michele's lack of understanding about the significance of carefully chosen words was the sole cause for the treatment failure, it undoubtedly contributed greatly to the lack of rapport developed, an important ingredient in successful treatment outcome. She could have avoided this failure by matching her client's label "discussion" instead of using her interpretation of the facts, "fight."

There are several aspects of matching clients' language we would like to discuss. The first simply requires that the therapist mirror the client's exact use of words or idiomatic expressions. Many times clients utilize particular pet phrases when talking about their difficulties. For example, a child or a marital partner may be described as having an "attitude problem." While we have never seen "an attitude" and are not certain what is meant by "an attitude problem," we will use the term "attitude" when inquiring further into its observable behavioral aspects. For example, we ask, "What is Sue doing differently when she has a good attitude? What will be the first sign that her attitude is improving?"

Similarly, when a client reports, "I want to look before I leap," we might summarize the session: "It makes good sense to be cautious, to look before you leap." Sometimes we note key phrases used by clients to portray their experiences and incorporate these phrases into messages we give them later.

Another aspect of mirroring or matching involves using clients' metaphors. Once, after having accomplished a great deal of change, a client said, "Things are much better now, but I anticipate a rocky road in the future." To this we later responded, "While we agree that there might be a rocky road up ahead, we are convinced that you now have a four-wheel drive vehicle to handle it."

Knowing about people's work or hobbies can also be extremely useful in developing metaphors to which they can relate easily.

Bill was once working with a man who wanted to stop dressing in women's clothing. He said that he had done it for so many years that, even though he wanted to change, ". . . you can't teach an old dog new tricks." Later in the interview, he happened to mention that one part of his life that was going very well involved his hobby of breeding some rare breed of dogs. Bill said that, since the man was an expert in the matter, Bill wanted to know, for the record, whether one could teach an old dog new tricks. The man unhesitatingly answered, "Yes." After that it was an easy matter to work on ways to teach this old dog to stop dressing in women's clothing.

Another example of using metaphors based on the client's work involved a man whose expertise was in the area of computers; he was a systems analyst. When the therapist referred to his client's relationship with his girlfriend (the reason he was seeking therapy), he used "computerese language," such as, "the system going down," "system overload," "garbage in, garbage out," and so on. The man felt understood, and rapport developed rapidly.

In the case of a 17-year-old alcohol abuser and former state wrestling champ, the therapist* utilized the client's love of wrestling and his competitive spirit to help him "wrestle control of his life." Due to his alcohol use, the boy had recently stopped participating on his wrestling team. The therapist first challenged his client by asking the provocative question, "How long are you going to allow this alcohol problem to push you around?" (Michael White, personal communication, 1987). Since the wrestler prided himself on his strength and virility, he responded with examples of times he was able to overcome the temptation to drink. From these reports of successful handling of the situation, and from his own experiences as a former wrestler, the therapist developed a most creative intervention. The client and his mother were given a daily ritual designed to help the young wrestler put the alcohol problem on its back. The client was instructed to keep track of the various things he did each day to avoid being pinned by the alcohol problem. At the end of each day, the client was to go to his mother to receive a score for his daily performance. (His mother attended most of his wrestling matches, so she was familiar

*Matthew Selekman, a former colleague of Michele's.

with the scoring system.) The client was given a special privi-
lege for pinning the alcohol problem, three points for a near
pin, two points for a reversal, and one point for an escape.
Several sessions later he had given up drinking, obtained a
job, and had gone out for wrestling for his senior year.

MATCHING SENSORY MODALITIES

Bandler and Grinder (1979) developed a technique that involves matching people's verbs and predicates with the sensory modality they are using. They noticed that some people use very visually oriented words, e.g., "I see what you mean," or "I can't quite picture that." Others use auditory words, e.g., "It sounds like things are going fairly well," or "I hear where you're coming from." Feeling words form a third category, e.g., "It feels as if I am going to explode sometimes," or "I have a feeling that this isn't going to work." It is as if clients speak specific dialects and have difficulty understanding and being understood by speakers of other dialects. Bandler and Grinder suggest that the therapist match the client's sensory modality words in order to indicate understanding and develop rapport. For example, if the client says, "I just can't *picture* myself doing that," the therapist might say, "So maybe we could take a closer *look* at that."

CHANNELING THE
CLIENT'S LANGUAGE

We initially use words that clients use and then start to channel the meanings for those words in productive directions or use different words. For instance, a mother who was seeing Bill for help with her daughter started the session by saying that her daughter had been hoarding newspapers. That was what brought them to therapy. When Bill asked more about the situation, initially he also used the word hoarding, but soon changed it to "keeping" or "collecting." After a time, both mother and daughter started using the words Bill used to describe the situation.

We find it useful to channel language away from jargon using fixed, negative labels towards action descriptions found in everyday language. Often when people seek therapy, they have already been "therapized," that is, they have become accustomed to using the concepts and jargon from some theory of psychology or therapy. Some of these they may have absorbed from previous therapists, as when a client of ours said to us once, "I guess I was coming from my critical parent at that moment" (this comes from transactional analysis). Some of these "trickle down" through the popular media. For instance, the idea of repression is a Freudian concept that has become an everyday part of our culture, and although it is just a theory it is accepted as a fact of life by most people in our culture. If you lived two hundred years ago, this would have been a very strange idea, incomprehensible to most.

When clients use negative, fixed labels to describe themselves or others, we translate those labels into descriptions of actions. When someone says that her husband is "narcissistic," we like to know what it looks like and sounds like when he is being "narcissistic." We find it much easier to deal with actions than with fixed characteristics. Further, as you will see, moving from fixed labels to action descriptions has the intended effect of depathologizing or normalizing clients' situations.

To a parent who remarks that her child is "school phobic," we might respond, "So, Steve hasn't been going to school lately," or, "Steve has been giving you a hard time about going to school." To an overeater who claims she has an "eating disorder," we might say, "So, sometimes you eat too much." Action descriptions depict things which are visible and therefore measurable. It's hard to recognize a diminish-

ing phobia or a reduction in narcissism unless there is agreement in advance about what that will look like.

Once we have joined the client through matching, we can
channel the conversation toward less pathological, more normal descriptions of the difficulty. The therapist can do much
to alter clients' perception of the problem by gradually modifying the label used to describe the troubling situation. For example, terms like "depression" are buzz words. The media are
replete with information about it. Clients describing themselves as "depressed" think that their problem is insidious, serious, and difficult, if not impossible, to resolve. To the extent
that we accept the clients' negative label, we make our therapeutic tasks considerably more difficult. Taking another tack,
in the case of "depressed" clients, we can begin to subtly shift
perceptions by asking, "Has anyone noticed that you have felt
'down in the dumps' recently?" Later, we might change "down
in the dumps" to "moodiness," implying that there are "up"
times in the cycle, or "discouraged," implying something less
disturbed and more common.

There are many other terms we use on a fairly regular
basis because of the normalizing effect they have on client's
perceptions. We often summarize at the end of a session,
referring to the client's troubled situation as a "transitional
period." We might say, "It is obvious to me that you already
have done several things to help yourself through this transitional period." Since transitional periods are time-limited,
clients take solace in hearing this and it helps shape their
expectations about their future. Similarly, we might also respond to a parent who describes his child as "immature" by
calling the child a "late bloomer." If clients return with continuing difficulties but have made some improvements in
their situation, we might discuss with them how to "fine
tune" their efforts, rather than giving up.

The careful use of verb tenses can create a reality where
the problem is in the past and possibilities exist for the
present and the future. For instance, when clients talk as if

they are still having their problems, we change the verb tenses when we reflect back to them what they have said. Our verb tenses reflect our view that at any moment the "problem" could dissolve or that it might not even exist. For example, if a client says, "I binge and vomit every day," we would probably say, in reflecting back to her what she has told us, "So you've binged and vomited every day for some time now." Our phrasing does not presume that she will continue to binge and vomit in the future or that she has always binged and vomited. This use of verb tenses is very much a part of creating a context for change.

The following excerpt from one of Michele's cases shows that an awareness of verb tenses can provide an opening for solutions that might not have been apparent before. In this case the client begins to talk about her problem using the past tense.

MICHELE   So, what brings you in?

CLIENT   Well, I've used counseling on and off and I do have problems with PMS. I do have little bouts of depression here and there, but I've learned to live with, kind of work through it. A couple of months ago I really started noticing that I was very unhappy at work and very unhappy at home. I really started trying to think, why am I so, . . . because I love my husband a lot and I respect him and like him. So, what else can you expect from a husband? My eight-year-old and I have some problems as a result of his chronic illness. I like him . . . periodically. (Laughter)

MICHELE   You like him periodically?

CLIENT   Yeah.

MICHELE   So what else is new?

CLIENT   Periodically I don't like him.

MICHELE   Well, so what else is new?

CLIENT   Um, things money-wise are fine. I drive a BMW. There really wasn't a lot in my life that I could complain about, but I couldn't figure it out. And it kind of . . . Jack and I lead very stressful . . . well, all America does, I guess. But we lead very busy lives. We both have supervisor positions, we're very busy and stressed. But I couldn't really figure out why . . . I figured out that I was mad at both of them [her husband and son] and I couldn't really figure out why. So, I finally, after a lot of thinking, I decided that I was really resenting Jack [her husband] because his life is, was, so stress-free and I have this "term paper syndrome" where I'd constantly worry if the dishes were done, if the laundry was done. It's not his fault, Jack helps very much. It was carrying the responsibility around in my mind.

MICHELE   He does help you?

CLIENT   (Emphatically) Oh yes, very much. I do initiate a lot of things but . . .

MICHELE   He pitches in.

CLIENT   Oh, oh yeah. I told him when I married him he would have to do his half or I would move out. (Laughter) So I was really resenting him for that fact and I was really resenting my son. He's a very manipulative kid and he can manipulate me without me even knowing it. Basically what I was resenting was that he was outsmarting me and I really didn't like that. Plus I realized that at home I make decisions based on guilt. I feel responsible if Jack isn't happy or if something happened. I feel responsible if Bill's [her son] life isn't wonderful and complete and I feel responsible . . . I just felt totally responsible for the things done . . .

MICHELE   Let me interrupt you for a second. You, when you're talking about all this, you're talking in the past tense. Have you since put some of this together?

CLIENT   Yes, well I have to some degree and it was really interesting. When I made the phone call and made the appointment it was kind of like of . . . We came to coun-

seling before and it triggered something in us that we
needed to really talk. And . . .

MICHELE   And you did that.

CLIENT   We are doing that. I don't think we are done . . .

MICHELE   You are never done.

CLIENT   No, but I mean, we are doing that.

MICHELE   Good.

CLIENT   I've made conscious . . .

MICHELE   How did you get that to happen?

CLIENT   Just by saying to myself that I am not going to live
like this . . . So, we are talking.

MICHELE   Okay. Are you feeling like you are starting to . . .

CLIENT   I feel a lot better today. I mean, last night. We got
into a point where we were both so tired from our jobs
that we weren't having enough sex, which is enough for
us. We kind of got ourselves into a vicious cycle. And I
think we have kind of gotten ourselves out. Last night
we made wonderful love and it was nice and we both
felt better.

MICHELE   Great. How did you get that to happen?

Most of the remainder of the session explored the solutions she had undertaken before she came in. Then there
was a discussion of what she needed to do to keep the
changes going and how she might make one or two additional small changes to make her situation really satisfying. At
the end of the session she thanked Michele and suggested
she might call some time in the future, but for now she felt
much better.

In reviewing the videotape of this session, it is apparent
how easy it would have been—if the therapist had not been
listening for solution language and possibilities—to have
missed the subtle language cues that the client had already
begun to resolve her situation. Exploring the inadequacies
of her relationship with her husband and/or her child is a

direction some therapists would have taken. That choice would have led to a very different first session.

Most clients do not, as in the case of Michele's client, start by describing their problems in the past tense. The therapist can begin to shift the talk, thereby shifting the thinking, by first matching the present and then altering to the past tense, even in the first session. The session can be used to create a distinction between that which happened before and everything else yet to come. For example, we might ask clients, "How did the 'old you' handle this kind of situation?" This "old you" designation precedes our client's referring to herself in this way.

Here is another example of this shift in the use of tense: After hearing, "I have difficulty making decisions . . . ," we might say, "So, you were having difficulty deciding on . . . ," or, later in the session, when even slight evidence of decisiveness surfaces, "When you used to get stuck making decisions. . . ."

Frequent use of the word "yet" also characterizes our work. "Although things aren't great yet, they are certainly going in the right direction," implies that eventually things will be great. A related concept is illustrated during Bill's hypnosis seminars. Bill asks participants if they can hear the difference between the following two questions: "Have you ever been in trance?" and "Have you been in trance before?" The latter implies that trance is imminent.

We demonstrate our confidence that goals will be reached when we ask questions using definitive terms vs. possibility terms. The following questions illustrate this technique:

> "What *will* be different in your life *when* the two of you are getting along better?" rather than "What *would* (or *might*) be different in your life if . . . "

> "Who *will* be the first to notice *when* you cut back on your drinking? instead of "Who *would* be the first to notice *if* you cut back on your drinking?"

"*When* Johnny has started getting better grades at school, what kinds of things *will* you as his parents be able to do that you have recently stopped doing due to your concern about him?" vs. "*If* Johnny were to start getting better grades at school, *would* there be anything you and your husband would like to do. . . ?"

We intentionally use possibility terms vs. definitive terms to challenge unhelpful certainties held by clients. For instance, to a woman absolutely convinced that her husband will criticize her best efforts, we might say, "*If* your husband doesn't appreciate the work that you have done, what *might* you do?" vs. "*When* your husband berates you, what *will* you do?"

Sometimes clients (and indeed therapists) talk in such a way as to close down possibilities and give the impression that nothing can change. If a client says, "I'll never get a job," when summarizing we might respond, "So far you haven't gotten a job. . . ." This is different from using positive thinking and cheerleading. We do not say, "Of course, you will get a job," but we speak in such a way as to keep the possibilities open for the present and the future. Likewise, to a person who has recounted a history of unsuccessful therapy, we would say, "So you haven't found the help you've wanted yet."

Many of the presuppositions discussed seem obvious as you now read them, yet rarely do clients object to or question them. In fact, they rarely seem to be consciously aware of them. The new attributions appear to "fit." And, if they don't quite "fit" yet, clients rapidly grow into them (just as a puppy's body grows to fit his huge paws). The therapeutic reality that is being continually created has made the possibility of success acceptable and even sensible.

Another way we typically create a context for change is to introduce new distinctions into clients' thinking (O'Hanlon, 1982b, 1987). Once these distinctions are introduced, it is difficult to forget them.

A client seeking help from a supervisee of Bill's said that his problem was that he was selfish. Bill had the supervisee say that there was "selfish" and "selfish," and he wanted to know which one the client was. The first kind of selfish was when one took care of oneself, but felt a little guilty because of thinking one was supposed to take care of everyone else first. The other kind of selfish was when one disregarded other people's needs and feelings, took advantage of others, etc. The client said he did not disregard other people's needs, but that he was perhaps too sensitive to other people's needs and took care of them without taking care of himself. Then he had no time or energy left for himself and his needs. So perhaps the first kind of selfish was what he meant. The therapist then said he called the first kind of selfishness, "self-caring." At this point, the client decided that perhaps he just needed to take better care of himself and didn't need therapy after all.

Sometimes the therapist can help clients make distinctions that would help change the view they have of their situations. A client who talks seriously about suicide can be given a talk about the difference between *thinking* about suicide, which many people do, or *feeling* like killing oneself, and actually *doing* something about those thoughts or feelings.

Bill had a client who was afraid to go very far from his home. One of his boundaries was a bridge that joined one city to another. He said that if he went across the bridge he felt like he would die. Bill discussed with him the difference between feeling like you were going to die and actually dying. This simple distinction helped the client confront his fear and cross the bridge.

Here, once again, we use language to introduce distinctions that will be helpful to clients and to eliminate distinctions that don't contribute to solutions.

5.

The Session as Intervention
The Components of
Solution-Oriented Interviewing

Before we start our discussion of the components of solution-oriented interviewing, we would like to remind our readers that each person or encounter is unique and cannot, in our view, be adequately dealt with by slavishly following any methods one finds in a book. We both teach therapy workshops and see clients and it has often occurred to us after giving a wonderful workshop (in which our clinical work appears to be brilliant and clear), that it is a shame our clients did not attend the workshop. They would then know how they were supposed to respond to our wonderful interventions!

Peggy Papp advised family therapists to be cognizant of the interactive nature of "brilliant interventions" (1984, p. 25). She writes, "Sometimes clients turn our most mundane interventions into transcendental experiences, . . . while at other times, they remain totally impervious to our strokes of genius. . . ."

Michele had to chuckle at a recent reminder of the severe limitations to "strokes of genius" which aren't truly interactive.

A family came to her agency two and a half years ago to receive help with their teenaged daughter. She was doing poorly in school and was having great difficulty getting along with her stepfather. Michele worked with them for several sessions with only a slight degree of success. They were presently returning to the agency with similar complaints.

Since the agency uses a team approach with a one-way mirror, Michele decided not to be the primary therapist, but to take a second chance with the family as a team member behind the mirror. Not all therapists are lucky enough to try again. After several sessions it was clear that the team was not having any more success than Michele had had several years ago. Everyone felt really stuck.

Finally, after several more weeks, Michele emerged from a corner of the dark room behind the mirror with a light bulb flashing over her head. The therapist and the team huddled around her during the consultation break, anxiously awaiting the missing key. Michele quietly and deliberately spewed out an elegant reframe, weaving together all the intricate family pieces. The team sighed with relief, making reassuringly flattering compliments about Michele's clinical aptitude. All that remained was for the therapist to deliver to the family "our gift."

The therapist returned to the therapy room and began to speak. The team waited breathlessly for the nonverbal messages — head nods, thoughtful glances and knowing smiles — signaling that "our gift" had been accepted by the family. The suspense was killing the team. As the therapist finished his soliloquy the stepfather said, "Michele Weiner-Davis told us that the last time we were here. I didn't buy it then and I don't buy it now." Oops! Is it really possible that a family can be impervious to "strokes of genius" twice?

Actually, the difference between our theories and our clients' behavior is what makes therapy new and challenging.

We view therapy as a bit like rock climbing. You have an idea of the goal, but the actual scaling of the mountain involves using general methods of rock climbing adapted to a particular mountain. Sometimes you may even have to break the rules of the accepted method to reach the goal. The mountain will "teach" you how to scale it. Likewise, clients have taught us how to help them reach their goals and sometimes they have taught us that it will take something other than our usual procedures to get there.

Another analogy we use to describe this process comes from the sport of curling. Curling is an ice sport wherein a puck (called a "stone") is shoved across the ice and players sweep the ice in front of the stone to help it go further and to channel it in the desired direction. Therapy for us is like that. Clients are going somewhere and we are constantly sweeping openings in front of them to help channel their thinking and actions in the direction of solutions and goals. It is merely a channeling, though, and if clients are headed in one direction and we are oblivious to where they are and start sweeping on the other side of the ice, we will lose our influence and credibility with them. We think it is important to acknowledge and validate what clients have been thinking and feeling and then, as quickly as possible, to help them think, feel, and act in more satisfying ways.

ASSESSMENT AS INTERVENTION

We have observed enough "one-session cures" to be utterly convinced that they are neither flukes, miracles, nor magic. Rather, something powerfully therapeutic occurs in the interaction between therapist and client during these sessions. We view the process of interviewing as an intervention; that is, through the use of various solution-oriented interviewing techniques, clients can experience significant shifts in their thinking about their situations during the course of the session. These shifts free people to leave our offices and act in more productive ways. In many cases, a task assigned at the end of the session merely serves to reinforce the change which has already occurred (O'Hanlon and Wilk, 1987).

Others in the psychotherapy field share a similar view about interviewing. In their paper entitled, "The Purposeful Interview," Eve Lipchik and Steve de Shazer (1986) describe several categories of questions. Some are designed to elicit information about the client's present framing of the complaint. Others are future-oriented questions designed to construct solutions and to create the expectation of change. The latter, called "constructive questions" share many similarities to the material we discuss here. Klaus Deissler (1986), Gunther Schmidt and Bernhard Trenkle (1985), therapists from Germany who have been influenced by both Erickson and the Milan family therapy approach, have also discussed the use of questions to introduce new information into family systems.

More recently, in an article called "Interventive Interviewing," Karl Tomm (1987) examined the role of what he calls "reflexive questioning." He described his experience as a team member observing from behind a one-way mirror. One particular session greatly influenced his thinking about the impact of certain kinds of therapeutic questions:

A family consisting of two parents and eight children sought therapy because of the father's violent tendencies in disciplining several of the children. In a very short period of the time it became apparent to the therapist and team that the parents could not agree on discipline methods, and that the children saw mother as loving and caring, while father was viewed as uncaring and unreasonable. As the children sided with their mother, father's tension appeared to build. Intended to be a tension-breaker, Tomm suggested the therapist ask each child: "If something were to happen to your

mother so that she became seriously ill and had to be hospi-
talized for a long time, or perhaps even died, what would
become of the relationship between your father and the rest
of the children?"

The first child feared that the father's violent tendencies
would only escalate. The second child said, "But he might
see another side of us because we would have to get him to
help us with our schoolwork." The rest of the children pro-
jected a warm, loving image of their father. The therapist
proceeded in a different direction once the children re-
sponded to the question.

During the consultation break the therapist and team
agreed on an intervention which would interrupt the pat-
tern of blaming and hostility. They positively connoted "the
father's uncaring, tyrannical behavior as helping the mother
and children to get closer and support one another (for the
time being) because he knew how much they would miss
each other when the children left home. On hearing this
opinion, the children immediately protested, saying that
their father was not uncaring or tyrannical. They insisted
that he was very affectionate and helpful!" (p. 168).

The obvious conclusion Tomm drew from this experience
was that the question to the children about the possible
effects of mother's absence offered them a new and different way to look at their father and their relationships with
him. In effect, the question was an intervention. This led
Tomm to think about other interviewing questions he utilized which appeared to have a similar "healing" effect.

PRESUPPOSITIONAL QUESTIONING

Presuppositional questioning is the name we have given
to the types of questions we ask during the session which are
designed to function as "interventions." By this we mean

that we intend to influence clients' perceptions in the direction of solution through the questions we choose to ask and
our careful use of solution language. Reflection upon these
questions helps clients to consider their situations from new
perspectives.

As we mentioned earlier, there is no answer to the question, "Have you stopped beating your wife?" that does not
incriminate. Presuppositional questions have a similar but
opposite effect; they direct clients to responses that are self-
enhancing and strength-promoting. In responding to these
questions, clients can't help but accept the underlying prem-
ise that change is inevitable. Interestingly enough, we have
noticed that sometimes the questions themselves are so
powerful in the distinctions they make during the session
that a response is not required for them to be effective. We
offer examples of this later.

There are times during the session when we are not asking presuppositional questions. For instance, we make statements ("That sounds different from the way you dealt with it
last week,") and ask neutral questions for informational pur-
poses ("Is next Thursday a good time for you?"). It is, however, our goal to use this subtle yet effective means of influence as often as possible.

A basic rule of thumb in constructing presuppositional
questions is to keep them open-ended, avoiding questions to
which a "yes" or "no" response would be possible. Instead of,
"Were there any good things that happened?" ask, "What
good things happened?" The latter question implies that the
therapist is certain that good things happened. Instead of,
"Did you ever do anything that worked?" ask, "What have
you done in the past that worked?" Again, the latter suggests
that inevitably there have been successful past solutions. For
instance, after a mother related 15 minutes of stories about
her teenage son's bad behavior, a therapist asked, "Did you
do anything to set limits for him?" To this, the mother simply

said, "No." The disadvantage of phrasing the question in a "yes" or "no" form is that it indicated to the mother that taking no action in response to bad behavior was within the realm of possibility. It does not presume that the mother is actively engaged in solution-oriented behaviors. If, on the other hand, the therapist had asked, "What did you do to let him know that his behavior was unacceptable?" he would have indicated his certainty that some form of limit-setting has taken place. When therapists do not use this principle and ask "yes" or "no" questions, their clients often opt for providing simple "yes" or "no" answers. Asking an open-ended question almost always provides a more complete and useful answer.

While we use presuppositional questioning as much as possible, the specific question we choose depends on our goal at any particular point during the session. There is a pattern to the order in which these questions are asked. The following section will offer examples of how and when to implement them in order to unveil solutions.

THE FIRST SESSION

" . . . most of our therapeutic successes can be attributed to the opening phases of psychotherapy. . . . Like chess, the game is either won or lost in the beginning."

— Richard Rabkin, *Strategic Psychotherapy*, p. 11

Joining

When we meet clients we usually spend the first few minutes chatting about anything but what might be considered the reason they are sitting in our office. We ask about what they do for employment, how they like their job, where they go to school, whether they work outside the home, the weather or the art work on the wall. Our goal during this joining period is to show nonjudgmental interest in them and help them feel comfortable. We use many of the joining techniques described in Chapter 4, avoiding confrontation and topics of conversation where disagreement is likely. The amount of time spent in this phase of therapy depends on how quickly clients appear to "loosen up."

A *Brief Description of the Problem*

Usually the next question is, "So, what brings you in?" Following a very brief problem statement, we ask a series of questions designed to extract information about exceptions to the problem — times when things are progressing smoothly, past solutions to the current problem, and the person's strengths and resources.

Exceptions to the Problem

It has been our observation that regardless of the magnitude or chronicity of the problems people experience, there are situations or times when, for some reason, the problem simply does not happen. Bed-wetters have dry nights, combative couples have peaceful days, teenagers sometimes comply with the rules without an argument, and so on. Most people, therapists included, consider these problem-free times to be disconnected from or unrelated to the problematic times and so little is done to better understand or amplify them. As we have already indicated, the exceptions to the problem offer a tremendous amount of information about what is needed to solve the problem. Solutions can be unearthed by examining the differences between times when the problem has occurred and times when it has not. Clients often simply need to do more of what is already working until the problem no longer exists.

The concept is so simple. If people want to experience more success, more happiness and less stress in their lives, help them assess what is different about the times when they are already successful, happy and stress-free. Therein lies the solution — increasing those activities which have a track record of having achieved (even for short periods of time) the desired goal.

Initially, a very interesting thing happens when we ask clients about exceptions. They often are quiet momentarily and appear to be lost in thought. The reason for this silence is that people generally cast the events in their lives in black and white terms: "You never are the one to make plans for us. I always do," or "He wets the bed all the time." Although it is unlikely that only one partner is "always" the planner and it is impossible that any person wets the bed "all the time," this, nevertheless, is the way people perceive it. So, when we ask, "What is different about the times when your husband does make plans for you?" or, "What is different about the nights when there are dry beds?", we are asking people to report on experiences they haven't really paid much attention to yet. All they have been noticing until now is slow social calendars, hurt feelings, wet beds, laundry, and frustration. They fail to notice or give significance to the occasional time when one spouse does ask the other out for lunch, or that morning last week when the bed was bone dry.

Another reason clients sometimes seem a bit unprepared when we ask the presuppositional question pertaining to exceptions is that they do not expect therapy to be a place where one discusses what is going right. Therapy is a place to talk about problems. After all, no TV or movie therapist ever asks about what is going right. In asking about exceptions, we are not only attempting to redirect people's attention to what is already working but also orienting people as to what we think is important to know and talk about in therapy.

Michele has observed another interesting phenomenon in regard to clients' problem-solving strengths and exceptions. Frequently, during the first session clients discuss changes they have made between the call for treatment and the first session. Typically, as with other exceptions, clients place little significance on these changes, since they are viewed as flukes. However, if clients are able to recognize that they have already begun to solve their difficulties prior to treatment, then the goals of therapy can be greatly simplified. Since clients have gotten the ball rolling, therapists merely need to keep it rolling, a considerably easier task.

On an informal questionnaire designed to survey clients seeking treatment at the McHenry County (Illinois) Youth Service Bureau, the following questions were asked:

1. Many times in between the call for an appointment for therapy and the first session people notice that already things seem different. What have you noticed about your situation?
2. (If changes were noted) Are these changes in the problem area?
3. (If changes were noted) Are these the kinds of changes you would like to continue to have happen?

Of the clients surveyed, two-thirds indicated that changes had been made prior to the first therapy contact. All of these clients answered "yes" to questions 2 and 3. Of the remaining one-third clients who initially indicated no pretreatment changes, it was quite common for them to remember those changes later in the session (Weiner-Davis, de Shazer, and Gingerich, 1987).

In discussing the notion of pretreatment change in workshops or with other colleagues, we have been offered further confirmation that this phenomenon is widely observed. It was exciting to note a case study in an international newsletter, the *Dulwich Centre Newsletter* published in Australia, which begins, "Have you ever noticed how many people are already getting over their problem by the time they consult you? And have you noticed that most of those people who are already successfully following their own solution didn't ever realize how well they were doing?" (Birch and Piglet, 1986, p. 10).

In addition to pretreatment change, many other examples of exceptions to the problem pattern are there for the asking. The following series of presuppositional questions illustrates more fully how to go about eliciting information about exceptions.

> 1. What is different about the times when _____ (you are getting along, there are dry beds, he does go to school, and so on)?

Here, any and all differences between problematic and nonproblematic times are explored. At first, some clients seem unable to think of any exceptions, but if we persist just a little, most clients eventually can describe a number of variables which characterize what is happening when the problem isn't. The key here is to assume a stance which indicates that you as the therapist would be surprised if there were no exceptions. If clients still appear baffled, to get the ball rolling we might suggest certain possibilities that might have accounted for things going smoothly.

Again, notice that we do not ask, "Have there been times when _____?" for this wording would not accomplish our goal of demonstrating our certainty that good things do happen. Additionally, the goal is always stated in positive terms. "When you are getting along" versus "when you aren't fighting." We want people to be thinking about getting along, not about not fighting. Not fighting still conjures up images of fighting (just as, for example, when one is told, "Don't let the picture of a purple flower enter your mind," a picture of a purple flower immediately comes to mind).

Workshop participants have asked, "How early in the session is too early to ask about exceptions?" Our response is that it is never too early; we usually ask about exceptions within the first few minutes of the session. It is important, though, to make certain that clients feel understood and validated. Some clients need to spend a bit more time than others explaining their situation before they shift gears.

When clients insist that there are never times that the problem doesn't happen, search for exceptions in a similar but related way, finding the best of the bad times. For example, ask, "When is it less severe, frequent, intense or shorter in duration?" or "When is it different in any way?" You might suggest absurd ideas to demonstrate that there are exceptions, asking things like, "Does it happen when you are sleeping?" Most people say, "Well, no, of course it doesn't." We are then on firmer ground when we ask about other nonproblematic times.

2. How do you get that to happen?

Once the client has reported even the slightest exception we ask, "How do you get that to happen?" On the simplest level this question gathers information about what the client has done to overcome the problem. Verbalizing this produces clarity both for us and for our clients. Once our clients identify how they get good things to happen, they will know what it will take to continue in this vein.

On a more subtle level, we are encouraging the client to take credit for whatever it is that is working. Since ordinarily clients do not assume credit, this presuppositional question frequently functions as an intervention. Even if the client outwardly denies the attribution initially and says, "I didn't do anything, he was just ready to change," we might suggest,

"You must have done something to stimulate his readiness. What could that have been?"

> 3. How does it make your day go differently when
> _____ (the exception happens)?"

This question suggests the interconnectedness between good things happening in one area of a person's life and good things happening in other areas. Although it is generally acknowledged that a bad day at work might lead to Mom's coming home and fighting with Dad, who then yells at his kid, who then kicks the dog, who then growls at the cat, and so on, people sometimes fail to see the connection between a *good* day at work and heightened pleasure in relationships with loved ones. This question affords people the opportunity to trace the positive impact that one small (or large) exception can have in their lives.

Notice, again, that the question is not, "Is there anything different about your day when . . . ?" Rather, we demonstrate our confidence that further worthwhile things happen when we ask, "How does your day go differently when . . . ?"

If there is more than one person present, each person could be asked this question. It can be very useful for family members to hear how a single positive action on the part of an individual affects the lives of others. This can be very reinforcing and serve to amplify that which is beneficial.

> 4. Who else noticed that _____ (you lost ten pounds,
> he did his homework, you got along well last week-
> end?) In what way could you tell that he noticed;
> what did he do or say?

This question has an impact similar to that of the one above. Furthermore, if there is more than one person in the session, they receive information about which of their behaviors are pleasing. This has obvious useful consequences for influencing future behavior.

> 5. How did you get her to stop _____ (throwing the temper tantrum, nagging)? How did you get the fight to end?

This question, asked when clients talk about the problem pattern, is tricky, in that it often requires thought before responding. Clients are focused on the fight, not the grounds of the settlement or the subsequent tranquility. Everyone can explain how fights begin. Clearly, if you have ever been in a relationship with someone, you know that fights begin because of something the other person did. "You started it!" is a common household battle cry. Explaining how fights end is a completely different story. This is generally a much more difficult endeavor — more difficult, but more important. For one thing, clients don't take (or give) credit for ending fights or temper tantrums. These disturbances are perceived as having a life of their own and dying by natural causes, when they are ready. In exploring this presuppositional question, "How do you get your fights to end?", clients begin to see a connection between something they do, and can do, and the cessation of an unpleasant occurrence.

For example, when a parent complains about a child's temper tantrums, the therapist's question could be, "How do you get the tantrums to end?" A common response is, "Eventually, when I am totally exasperated, I give up and just ignore him. Shortly after that he stops." Typically, people do not view ignoring as a solution, but as an unhealthy and frustrating capitulation. This view could be altered by asking, "How did you figure out that, in order to solve your problem and end the tantrums, you needed to ignore him? That's pretty clever." Even if the client denies having intentionally and logically arrived at the solution, we have given him or her credit for having done so. Furthermore, the question serves as a clear suggestion about a future course of action to limit tantrums.

> 6. How is that different from the way you might have handled it _____ (one week, one month, etc.) ago?

This question, asked whenever clients report anything which appears to be new or different, is an extremely important therapeutic tool since, as we have mentioned, many times clients do not recognize their own movement toward solution. It is quite common for clients to say, "Well, I guess it is different. I guess I handled the situation better this week than last week because I wasn't wishy-washy like before." For many, had the question not been asked, the "new behavior" would have gone unnoticed and therefore remained a difference that did not make a difference.

We speculate that it is not always the case that the "new behavior" is actually "new"; rather, in response to this question, the behavior is being observed and labeled as "different" for the first time and, therefore, is now a difference that makes a difference. Clinically, making this distinction is an invaluable step to constructing solutions, since future solution-enhancing behaviors are more likely to be noticed by clients. During the course of therapy, having been asked this question several times, clients beat us to the punch and tell us the ways in which the present challenges in their lives are being handled more effectively than in the past.

It is important to note here that when we say that we reinforce "anything positive" we mean *anything*. It does not have to be an exception to the problem pattern, nor does it even have to appear to be related to the problem. For that matter, the connection to the solution sometimes is not readily apparent. The information is stored to be used later when the connection becomes more obvious. Basically the goal is spotting and encouraging healthy trends. The following clinical example illustrates this technique:

One day Michele was supervising another staff member at her agency by reviewing a videotape of his work. His clients were a mother and her 15-year-old daughter. The presenting problem was that the girl had great difficulty getting herself up in the morning to go to school and, as a result, was truant quite often. The school was putting pressure on the mother to force her daughter to attend school. Mom's perspective was that nothing she did with her daughter ever worked; she was powerless. No matter how she tried, her daughter only did what she pleased.

To substantiate Mom's position even further, later in the session she cited more evidence of her daughter's defiant tendencies—she said that the girl didn't want to come for therapy at all. The therapist went on to discuss the details of the waking up problem. Michele asked the therapist if he had thought of asking Mom, "How in the world did you manage to get her here today since she didn't want to come and she usually does as she pleases?" He said that it was a passing thought, but since he couldn't see how it related to the problem of getting out of bed and truancy, he rejected the idea of asking it.

Although this therapist effectively inquired about exceptions to the problem pattern, either times when Mom was successful at getting the girl up and moving or times when the girl got herself up and out the door, he was uncertain as to how Mom's taking charge of getting the girl to the therapy appointment might be a similarly worthwhile focus. Focusing on Mom's effective parenting skills in general might introduce some doubt about her "powerless" self-concept. Her ability to take charge could then be transferred to the morning bedroom situation.

Sometimes the healthy trends solution-oriented therapists identify and encourage have less obvious connections to the presenting problem. In fact, superficially they often appear to be distinctly separate categories of behavior. However, as we mentioned before, we have found that anything clients are doing that is good for them warrants attention.

> 7. What do you do for fun? What are your hobbies or interests?

Often we search for the abilities and know-how needed to solve the problem in other contexts in the client's life. It may be that the client has some hobby or occupation at which she excels.

A woman who came in to see Bill was upset with her husband and the way he interacted with her. She attributed the problems in their relationship to his moodiness and felt helpless to do anything that would alter this. She happened to be a very skilled horse trainer, one whose expertise was often sought to train "impossible-to-train" horses. Bill asked her what her secret was for training "impossible-to-train" horses. She brightened considerably and proceeded to give him a lucid account of the principles of horse training. Bill took notes, as he quickly saw not only that she could use her know-how from the horse area in her marriage, but also that he could use these same principles in psychotherapy with good result. Here are the principles she elucidated:

> *1. Be consistent.*
> *2. Reward small changes and progress.*
> *3. Give up some small controls to keep the overall control (e.g., let go of one of the reins if the horse is fighting you).*
> *4. Do not get discouraged. Don't get hooked in unhelp-*

*fully (e.g., getting angry). If you do get hooked in,
stop the session and start fresh another time.*

*Bill told her that she should pretend that her husband was a
horse, but not to tell him as he might take it the wrong way.
She went off with new enthusiasm and ideas about making
changes in her marriage.*

>   8. Have you ever had this difficulty in the past? (If yes)
>   How did you resolve it then? What would you need
>   to do to get that to happen again?

With this question we are asking about past solutions to
the present difficulty, since sometimes all the client needs to
do is reapply a previous solution. People erroneously think
that if they eliminated a problem for a certain period of time
by applying a particular solution, but eventually the same or
a similar problem developed, then the original solution was
ineffective. We do not agree.

Instead, our observation is that, once the solution is working, people tend to relax and return to their old, less effective ways of handling the situation. Or they get busy and
forget the old solution they used successfully. Lo and be-
hold, the problem pops up again. When this happens, they
simply need to remember what worked and do it again. For
example, most therapists have heard parents say, "When I
am consistent and stick to my guns, he follows the rules.
When I ease up, he starts screwing up again." Would you
then conclude that consistency is not a valuable approach?
Of course not, you would probably just suggest reinstituting
a program of consistency.

Michele has learned this lesson firsthand with her seven-
year-old daughter, Danielle. Over the years Michele has observed one method which works exceedingly well in getting
Danielle to cooperate at home, whether the issue be dress-

ing for school, bed making, taking "no" for an answer, doing chores, or whatever. Together they create a chart which delineates each responsibility adjacent to a corresponding box in which a check or a star can be placed if so deserved. "Good behavior" warrants a check or a star. For some reason, Danielle has always thoroughly enjoyed this plan and it has always worked.

Once in a while Danielle, like most seven-year-olds, reverts to annoying behaviors. The only problem is that, before remembering to pull out the old chart routine, Michele usually tries many ineffective means — threatening, yelling and screaming, time-outs and so on. Eventually, sometimes days and months later, she reminds herself to do what once worked and Danielle predictably responds positively. (Physician, heal thyself!) The challenging part is simply catching oneself in the midst of knee-jerk responses, recalling the way to more serene times, and then doing it.

Once clients identify past solutions, we ask, "What would you need to do to get that to happen again?" On one level, we are asking whether the situation has changed in such a way that there would be obstacles to reapplying the solution. If so, how might these obstacles be overcome? If not, it is indirectly suggested that they do just that — reapply the previous solution.

Normalizing and Depathologizing

If pressed to speculate about the cause of many difficulties that motivate people to seek therapy, we would say that these difficulties have come about from some random events that just stuck around long enough to become viewed as a problem. We tend to view these things not as pathological manifestations but as ordinary difficulties of life.

One of the main general directions in which we channel the session is toward viewing things in the client's or family's situation as normal, everyday matters rather than as psychological or pathological issues. This "normalizing" of the behavior and experiences can be done straightforwardly by saying something like, "Well, that's pretty understandable," and then putting the situation they might have presented as psychological or pathological in an everyday frame of reference. We tend to offer commonplace explanations at every opportunity and a great many of the client's "news items" are shrugged off as simply "not newsworthy."

This approach is well known to physicians in general practice, who often reassure their patients less by what they say than by what they don't seem to regard as even worth remarking upon. When you complain to your doctor about headaches, it is usually reassuring that she does *not* mention brain tumors or CAT scans.

When therapists normalize the difficulties clients bring to therapy, clients seem relieved. Imagine the calming effect when the "expert" appears unruffled by your description of the problem. This reaction influences clients to think that perhaps things aren't as bad as they had thought. This is an area where it is perhaps best to communicate indirectly, by what is *not* said, by what one remains unruffled about. The most common way we normalize during the session is to say things such as, "Naturally," "Of course," "Welcome to the club," "So what else is new?" and, "That sounds familiar," when people are reporting things they think are unusual or pathological. For example:

CLIENT   So, when I grounded him, he stayed home and complained about it.
THERAPIST   Naturally. But he did stay home?
CLIENT   Yes.
THERAPIST   Good. (Therapist then changes the subject.)

or as in this excerpt:

CLIENT   My eight-year-old and I have some problems as a
result of his chronic illness. I like him . . . periodically.
(Laughter)
MICHELE   You like him periodically?
CLIENT   Yeah.
MICHELE   So what else is new?
CLIENT   Periodically I don't like him.
MICHELE   Well, so what else is new?

In our observations of therapists who don't incorporate
this ongoing normalizing feedback, we have noticed that
clients assume that they really do have a problem. Since
silence on the part of the therapist can help to reify the
problem, it is important to actively reframe the situation as
normal.

There are, however, more indirect ways of normalizing. .
We may tell anecdotes that place the client's situation in a
normal context, anecdotes from our own or our friends' experience. Particularly useful are stories by which we can
suggest, "Yeah, me too." Parents who characterize their child
as "immature" might be told a story about how the therapist
seemed as a child to be immature but was really a "late
bloomer" who turned out more mature and successful in the
end than some of his more "mature" and precocious peers.

*Bill used the "Yeah, me too" method of normalizing effec-
tively with a man who initially sought help in reducing his
high blood pressure. He also mentioned casually in the first
few minutes that maybe the high blood pressure was causing
the impotence he had recently been experiencing. After
several sessions, his blood pressure was down and he was
satisfied that it would remain so. Bill asked if there was
anything else that he was concerned about. He then discussed his concern about his impotence, a topic he had felt
too embarrassed to emphasize at first, but which was really a*

bigger concern than the high blood pressure. Bill talked with him about the possibility of doing hypnosis for this and/or participating in therapy with his wife.

In the course of this discussion, Bill mentioned that this was a common occurrence for men. In fact, Bill himself had been impotent at times and had found that the more he worried about it, the worse it got. Finally, he knew enough to just relax and concentrate on enjoying himself sexually, rather than striving to get an erection. He had not had the problem for any length of time since then.

When the man came back for the next session, he said that hypnosis was unnecessary because he no longer had a problem with impotence. When asked what had made the difference, he said that hearing that Bill had had the same problem made him feel it wasn't really irreversible and that he wasn't as strange as he had thought he was. When Bill happened to meet the man and his wife several months later, she blushed and thanked Bill for the help he had given her husband, leaving Bill with the impression that things had continued in a positive direction.

Another approach to normalizing is to interrupt the client's description of a situation and proceed to finish the story with some details that we can fill in from working with other people and from our own experience with similar situations. To anticipate the pattern the client is about to describe (e.g., "Don't tell me — the more you try to get it out of your mind, the harder it gets not to think about it") can, again, implicitly normalize the subject of that report.

One way to anticipate the client's situation is through the multiple-choice questions we ask, clearly revealing knowledge of a familiar kind of pattern. It can be quite a powerful and reassuring intervention to ask the parents of a child with temper tantrums, "Does he ever do this?" and then proceed to give a pretty good description of that child's behavior. If parents somberly report, for example, that their child in anger says, "I want to be unhappy," or "I wish I was dead!" we usually ask, "Have you heard any of these yet?: 'I hate you,' 'I wish you weren't my parents,' . . ." and so on, running through a whole list of the kinds of things kids say in anger. When we correctly identify one after the other, the context changes to one in which we and the parents can smile or laugh with recognition. Often parents add others to the list. This may also have the effect of inoculating the parents for any future tantrums — they've heard it all before.

An indirect approach used to suggest that behavior(s) which are alarming or upsetting to clients may be fairly normal is to first inform the client, "I am a bit confused," and then ask the question. "How can you tell the difference between your daughter's depression [which the parent fears] and normal teenage moodiness?"; " . . . between his being quiet because he is mad at you [which the wife believes] or his being quiet because he is just thinking about his day?" In effect, we are introducing uncertainty into beliefs that are not particularly helpful. We are challenging the negative or pathological interpretations clients make about their lives and the people around them.

The question, "How can you tell the difference between (the stated problem) and (a normalized explanation of it)?" really requires no response to be effective. Once the distinction has been made by means of the asking the question, the next time the situation arises clients typically wonder whether they have, up until now, been overreacting. Even when clients offer evidence for their position, e.g., "I know my daughter is depressed because her friends don't act like this with their parents," that does not mean that the question has been ineffective in shifting perceptions; generally, a seed has been planted.

To emphasize the role of the client's actions in the complaint and to normalize it we sometimes give a "recipe" for the complaint. We either tell the client the recipe or get them to teach us how to "do their problem."

Bill has a typical monologue he uses with clients who ask for therapy for depression. He says that he has seen many people who did really good depressions and has learned from the best. If he were going to do a really good depression, he would reduce the amount of stimulation from the environment and from inside himself. Perhaps he would go to his bedroom, pull the shades, and stay under the covers. Or maybe he would stay at home reading the same kinds of books (probably romance novels or self-help books, nothing that stimulated the mind or provided new ideas). If he talked to anyone, it would be the same person or people everyday, usually about the same topic (probably how miserable he was). But it would be essential to avoid anything that made him breathe deeply or move physically, because it is difficult to maintain a good depression that way. In addition, he would dwell on the past and all the things he should or shouldn't have done. He would compare himself with other people and lose by the comparison (e.g., he was too short, too fat, too skinny, not successful enough, not as sane). He would think that he had always felt this way and would always feel this way in the future, etc. By the time he is through with this litany, most people are smiling or nodding with recognition. They do not realize that they have inadvertently accepted the definition of depression as a "doing" and, therefore, as something they can do something about. From there, if that intervention has not been enough, it is a simple matter to ask the person which technique he or she specializes in and to use that as a focus for intervention.

Bill recently asked a client complaining of a weight problem to teach him what to do to gain weight with her method because he had been skinny all his life. She reported that he should eat as if he were on a diet all day — skip breakfast, eat

*only salads with no dressing at lunches — and then lose con-
trol and eat any goodies that were available at the office and
sneak snacks, like ice cream, late at night. Bill called this her
"Scarsdale Dairy Queen" diet. He agreed that it was a perfect weight-gaining strategy and told her that the depriva-
tion part of the diet seemed to be essential, so that one
would develop a ravenous hunger for quick calories like
sweets. Perhaps, he suggested, there might be a way to introduce a little more planned indulgence in her diet as a way to
avoid the "compulsive" bingeing on sweets.*

Later in this chapter, we will go into greater detail about
the use of compliments during and at the end of the session.
However, since this section covers the scope of normalizing
techniques, we want to mention normalizing compliments,
which are often particularly effective in offering clients a
new, healthier perspective on their situations.

Many times clients do not realize that the problems and/
or anguish they experience are simply a natural and normal
response to life events. Grieving follows a loss, chaos thrives
in homes filled with children, major adjustments follow the
birth of a child, tension and worry characterize financially
unstable families, and so on. Sometimes external events create challenges which are difficult to overcome. When clients
have trouble getting their lives in order, they typically resort
to blaming and self-deprecation, which only adds to the
problem, rather than appreciating the impact that external
events have had on their lives.

Since we think that many of the difficulties clients bring
to therapy are an expectable by-product of life circumstances or transitions, we might say something like, "Based
on everything you are telling me about the changes in the
past few months, I'm surprised you are doing as well as you
are;" or, "Given the fact that you are a single mother who is
very conscientious about her children, and that you have no

emotional support, I am very impressed that you are managing as well as you are;" or, "Seeing as how your mother died just two months ago, it is amazing how resilient you really have been." Clients usually look relieved when they hear this.

Sometimes, in order to normalize the presenting problem in the form of a compliment, we take the things clients say out of context. We emphasize some particular aspect of the situation which they have mentioned only in passing. For example, if a wife says, "I know all marriages have their ups and downs, but we have been fighting too much lately," we might give her a compliment at the end of the session, saying, "I am very impressed that you recognize that all marriages have their ups and downs. Some people naively think that married life should be blissful at all times. You, on the other hand, are more realistic." Or, if a mother says, "I know I should let go of my daughter and permit her to spread her wings, but it is really much too difficult for me," we might later compliment her, saying, "I am impressed that you know the importance of giving your daughter the opportunity to become more independent. Some mothers don't recognize this and cling excessively to their relationships with their daughters."

WHAT NEXT?

It is our goal during the session to focus our clients' attention on exceptions, solutions and strengths as much as possible. Concomitantly, we continually normalize their experiences, both directly and indirectly. In many cases, a combination of the techniques described above comprises the majority of the first session. If all goes according to plan, goal-setting is what occurs next.

Goal-setting

Throughout this book we have emphasized the future, goal-oriented focus of solution-oriented therapy. While it is clients' responsibility to tell us about the changes they wish to see occur, we take a very active role to assure that the goals are attainable and, hopefully, concrete enough so that we will know when we get there. This goal-setting procedure is very definitely a cooperative negotiation process. Our active role in this aspect of therapy maximizes the chances that clients will accomplish the goals constructed.

One of our cardinal rules in goal-setting is to start small. We ask: What will be the very first sign that things are moving in the right direction? If several exceptions were noted during the session, a more appropriate presuppositional question would be, "What will be a sign that things are continuing in the right direction?" This will also help to reinforce the notion that change has already taken place.

Since one of our basic assumptions is that a small change leads to additional changes, the logical place to start is with a first small step. If one person in a relationship changes, the relationship changes. If one family member changes, other family members also change. A change in one aspect of an individual's life leads to changes in other areas as well. As Erickson said, "Therapy is often a matter of tipping the first domino" (Rossi, 1980, Vol. 4, p. 454).

When we ask about goals, some clients respond with utopian or unrealistic first signs. They offer what they might ultimately like to see as an end goal. For instance, if a student has been receiving F's and D's in school, parents might say that the first sign of change would be his raising his grades to A's and B's. While this might eventually happen, it is essential to help these parents acknowledge the change process earlier by designating a smaller step as the first sign of change. We might ask, "Naturally, you would like for him to receive A's and B's. However, would his improving his grades to at least C's be the first sign he was getting there?" "Would the regular completion of his homework be among the first signs he is getting there?" Usually clients agree with that idea. This negotiation process is essential if treatment goals are to be accomplished.

Another important aspect of goal setting is that the goals must be *concrete*. Goals such as "more self-esteem," "more intimacy," and "feeling happier" are only starting points in the goal-setting negotiation process. When clients offer vague goals, such as, "I want to have more self-esteem," we respond, "Okay, good. What will you be doing differently when you have more self-esteem?" (Notice the use of solution language in the use of "will" rather than "would" and in the phrase "doing differently," which suggests concrete observable actions.) The goals should ideally be observable things—things people do or say. In workshops, Bill talks about video descriptions—things you would see and hear with a video camera. Therapists make their jobs more difficult when they accept ambiguous goals at the outset and then proceed, assuming they know what the client means.

An application of the principles outlined above is illustrated by a case of Michele's. A mother brought her 13-year-old daughter for therapy because, according to mother, "she is depressed."

MICHELE   What will be the first sign that Mary is feeling good again?

MOTHER   I know her really well and I can just tell by looking at her how she feels. (Parents are particularly good at this.)

MICHELE   I'm sure you can, but how would I know by watching her that she is in good spirits?

MOTHER   She would play the piano again.

MICHELE   Doesn't she play the piano at all?

MOTHER   Well, I guess she plays sometimes.

MICHELE   (Sensing mother's impatience with the specificity of the questions) Forgive me for being so picky. I am really a concrete person and the information you are giving me is helping quite a bit. How often does she play the piano now?

MOTHER   (Relaxing) Once or twice a week.

MICHELE   How many more times would she need to play for you to think that she is starting to feel better?

MOTHER   One or two more times a week.

MICHELE   (Summarizing) Okay, so when she plays the piano three or four times a week, you will know that things are getting better.

The daughter, having heard what her mother considered to be a sign of change, went home and played the piano a couple of more times that week. Mother, seeing her doing that, assumed that her daughter must be feeling better. Mother then relaxed because she thought that her daughter's alleged depression reflected on her own parenting skills. Since mother was more relaxed, she responded to her daughter in new ways, which led to even further changes in their relationship and in the girl's state of well-being.

The Break

An important part of working with teams and one-way mirrors is taking the consultation break, as at Milan, BFTC and MRI.* This allows the therapist and the team behind the mirror to convene and share ideas about the direction of

---

*It is crucial to note here that, while working within a team is fun, stimulating, and revitalizing, it is not necessary for successful outcomes. Solution-oriented therapy works equally well when working solo.

the case. Michele, who over the years has spent more time than Bill working with a team, has incorporated the break into all of her work with clients, even in her private practice where there is no mirror and no team. After three-quarters of an hour she informs clients that she likes to take what she calls her "think break" and steps outside for a few minutes to collect her thoughts about what her clients have told her. During the break she decides which aspects of the entire interview warrant highlighting during the subsequent feed-back portion of the session.

After waiting several minutes for the therapist to return, clients eagerly anticipate the therapist's perspective on their situation. The break, which serves as a context marker, al-lows the therapist to reemphasize points made during the session or to leave clients with new thoughts before their departure. When set apart from the rest of the session, the message to the client is seen as important and conclusive. Sometimes clients joke and ask, "So what's the verdict?" In this case, the "verdict" is a summary of things done well, compliments, normalizing comments, new frames of refer-ence, and finally, a prescription or assignment.

Compliments

As we mentioned earlier, we take every opportunity to spot and highlight positive trends. When we hear something a client is doing that is positive or solution-promoting, we make a mental note to compliment him or her about it. Bill does this in a casual way during the session, "Boy, it sounds like you have been handling the situation very well," and then proceeds with the interview. Although Michele high-lights the positive during the session by asking, "How is that different from before?" she is more likely to reserve until the end of the session the compliment, "I am really struck with all the good things you are doing for yourself in spite of the fact that things have been rough."

Generally, when providing feedback, the therapist reflects back to clients what they have already done to begin to solve the problem. Knowing what not to do in order to avoid having a problem is also something worth commenting on at this time.

If, during the course of the session, the client mentioned a future plan which sounds worthwhile, even if it was only casually mentioned, the therapist will note, "Your plan to _____ is really a good one. It demonstrates your good sense about things."

Another bit of positive feedback is the use of reframing or positive connotation (Boscolo, Cecchin, Hoffman, and Penn, 1987). Sometimes when it has been difficult to elicit exceptions to the problem during the session, clients' views about the situation can still be altered by giving the problem description new meaning. This can be accomplished through use of positive connotation, that is, ascribing positive intent and motivation to behaviors which have previously been considered problematic.

So, for example, a father who intervenes and interferes when the mother is disciplining her son might be told, "I am struck with your willingness to protect your wife's relationship with your son. When you step in as you do, you prevent her from being the 'bad guy' and take that responsibility on yourself. You must be fairly selfless in this regard." Or, to the adolescent who sat through the session in complete silence with his arms folded, "I am impressed at the faith you have in your parents to tell your side to the story. Most kids your age interrupt just to make sure I get the story straight."

In total, four or five compliments are usually given. Clients' nonverbal responses are carefully observed, and interaction is kept to a minimum. Clients are encouraged to respond only if what they want to say expands on positive issues being raised. The intervention follows the compliment section and is the last item of business other than rescheduling if necessary. (Chapter 6 focuses on intervention design.)

Back to the Future: Fast-forward Questions

Not all first sessions proceed smoothly. Sometimes clients are unable to identify exceptions or past solutions. (We want to emphasize however, that eventually most clients *are* able to find at least a few exceptions to the difficulty or one or two positives about their lives. This might take a bit of persistence on the part of the therapist, but it usually pays off.)

When exceptions cannot be recalled, and there seem to be no present or past solutions to capitalize upon, the next step is to ask future-oriented questions. Clients are asked to envision a future without the problem and describe what that looks like. Once the client describes the future without the problem, he has also described the solution. We call these "fast-forward questions."

One way to do this is to ask a variation of the miracle question, developed at BFTC. "If a miracle happened and you woke up tomorrow and your problem was solved, what will be different?" Bill sometimes uses a different version: "If I pulled out a magic wand and were able to perform magic on your situation, what will be happening that is different from before?" Both questions elicit information about what the solution will look like.

Since many times people haven't envisioned the future with the problem solved, this often proves to be a useful exercise. It appears that the mere act of constructing a vision of the solution acts as a catalyst for bringing it about. Further, through our use of the word "will" we are implying that a solution is imminent.

The following excerpt is from a first session of one of Michele's cases. A mother and her eight-year-old daughter, Pat, came for therapy because, from Mom's perspective, "She just won't listen to me." It illustrates the use of the miracle question, as well as demonstrating how to remain focused on the solution rather than on the problem.

MICHELE   If you went to sleep tonight and a miracle happened so that when you woke up tomorrow your difficulties disappeared, what will be different?

MOM   I wouldn't be yelling as much.

MICHELE   Okay.

PAT   And you wouldn't lose your voice.

MICHELE   What would you be doing instead of yelling?

MOM   We'd be probably spending more time together, doing things together.

MICHELE   Okay, like the kind of things you were just mentioning? (Referring to an earlier segment of the session)

MOM   Yeah.

PAT   Playing cards and stuff. You know we play cards only when I'm good.

MOM   That's because you only come up to me at the craziest times and want to play cards.

PAT   (Giggles)

MOM   Two minutes before bed, "Do you want to play cards with me?"

MICHELE   Isn't that the way it always goes? (Pat still giggling)

MOM   But it's real hard because there are some days when I come home from work and I've had it up to here with people . . . (she points to her head)

MICHELE   Sure, sure . . .

MOM   . . . and she'll start in immediately.

MICHELE   Mom, you want to play cards?

MOM   Yeah, not only that but . . .

PAT   Can I have this, can I have that?

MICHELE   Yeah right. (Smiling at the girl's precociousness)

MOM   (Smiling too) She knows, she knows what she does wrong but she keeps doing it.

MICHELE   Okay, . . . so this miracle just happened . . .

MOM   Okay.

MICHELE   And you just came home from work.

PAT   She just walked through the door.

MICHELE   What will happen instead?

PAT   (Bubbly and smiling) Hi Mom!

MOM   Yeah!!

MICHELE   And then??

MOM   You'll help me make dinner. She's a pretty good helper in the kitchen when she wants to be. And then after dinner we will clear the table, do any homework that has to be done.

PAT   I never clear the table . . . well sometimes.

MOM   You do too. You take your plate and put it in the sink.

PAT   One time I didn't.

MOM   Well . . .

MICHELE   But you do most of the time?

PAT   (Nods her head "yes") That's one of my chores.

MICHELE   So, you'd be cleaning up together and what will you be doing after that?

PAT   Fun things.

MOM   Well depending on whether it was bath night or not . . .

MICHELE   If not?

MOM   We'd probably be coloring or playing with dolls instead.

Notice that once Mom projected into the future she had positive things to say about Pat—that she is a good helper in the kitchen and that she does put her plate in the sink. Several sessions later, when the problem was resolved, they reported doing the exact things they described in their miracle, a miracle come true!

Sometimes, when people describe their miracle the therapist can ask, "Are there small pieces of this that are already occurring?" This renews the search for exceptions. "What do you need to do to make it happen more?" is the next logical question (Lipchik, 1988). Also, the therapist makes certain that the client has a fairly good idea about which small steps need to be taken before the miracle can be realized. So, for instance, we will ask a young woman who mentions that when the miracle happens she will be back in college: "What do you need to do to re-enroll?" "Where do you get the application?" "How can you be certain to get the application in on time?" And so on.

In addition to questions about miracles and magic, there is a series of other future-oriented questions that appear to have a hypnotic effect on clients. These questions require that clients not only imagine a future without the problem but also fill in all the details of future scenes in which they are the main actors. The more specific the questions, the more complete the painted picture. The therapist simply assumes the problem has been resolved and asks about all the changes that will occur as a result.

- "How will your life be different?"
- "Who will be the first to notice?"
- "What will he do or say?"
- "How will you respond?"

To someone who has had a fear of flying:

- "What will it be like to get off the plane at your destination?"

- "How will you feel about yourself for having accomplished the flight?"
- "Who else will notice the self-confidence you will feel?"
- "What will your friends on the other end say to you when you arrive?"
- "How do you think your vacation will go, knowing that you have overcome your discomfort about flying?"

To someone with a weight problem:

- "When you lose 15 pounds, which will be your favorite store to buy new clothes?"
- "Will you need dresses or slacks? What colors are you most likely to choose?"
- "What will your husband say when you come home with a new wardrobe?"
- "Will your mother or father comment about the new thin you first?"

This is only a small sample of the questions that can be asked. The structure of the questions varies from client to client because the details in each question must "fit" the specifics of the person's situation. Basically, we are asking clients to fantasize about their future in a specific and pleasant way. (A case study at the end of this chapter further depicts the use of these "fast-forward" questions.)

Asking About the Problem

If clients are not able to describe exceptions, or to answer future-oriented questions, the next tack is to gather detailed information about the problem. The MRI brief therapy approach is most recognizable when we take this particular direction. Most of our cases do not require this sort of questioning, since we generally acquire enough information about exceptions and strengths to initiate the solution process. When inquiring about the problem, we are interested in very specific information: clients' frames of reference about the problem; how they see it as a problem; and the circumstances and the sequence of events when the problem occurs. We typically ask the following questions:

- "What do you see as the problem? Give me a recent example of it."
- In tracing the sequence of events we ask, "What happens? ... Then what happens? ... After that, what happens?" and so on until we have a clear picture of the interactions surrounding what is being called the problem. We want to know how clients have been trying to solve the problem (attempted solutions).
- "Who is present when the problem happens?"
- "What does each person say or do?" "And then what happens?"
- "Where does the problem most frequently occur?"
- "Where is it least likely to occur?"
- "Is there a particular time (of day, month, year) when the problem is (un)likely to happen?"
- "How is it a problem for you?"
- "If your wife were here now, how would she say that you are trying to solve the problem?"

Even when we become problem-focused during the session, we are in no way attempting to understand "the real meaning of the problem," to find its "cause" or to pursue any other similar notions about problem-solving. Only those aspects of the problem that provide us with the kind of information we need to formulate useful interventions are of interest. For example, it is clear from Erickson's work that any change in the pattern surrounding the problem may decrease the likelihood that the problem will happen. Therefore, once we have a clear picture of the sequence of events when the problem happens, we can suggest a small change that might make a significant difference.

Another way of inquiring about the problem pattern is based on the work of MRI. As previously mentioned, they see problems as being maintained through people's unsuccessful problem-solving attempts. Consequently, what is needed to solve the problem is to reverse the problem-solving effort. Once we have a detailed understanding of the unsuccessful problem-solving efforts, we can suggest to clients that they reverse the way in which they have been handling the situation.

Occasionally, when we are finding out about the problem sequence an exception emerges. We promptly ask about it and, if this direction appears to be fruitful, i.e., leads to further information about exceptions, the problem-focused inquiry is abandoned.

Searching for Strengths and Solutions as "More of the Same"

Therapists often ask us, "Don't you have clients who want to show you how awful things are, particularly when you are being positive? Doesn't going after exceptions occasionally bring out the worst in clients?" Yes, of course there are times when we notice that our being positive leads to clients' being negative. This has impressed upon us the importance of watching people for their responses and then modifying our actions if necessary.

In supervising therapists who are just learning the solution-oriented approach, we notice a common error—a rigid focus on positives even though the client continually disqualifies the positives both verbally and nonverbally, i.e., "Sure he did his homework but that's only a drop in the bucket," or "Yes, her behavior was better this week, but she has pulled this 'good routine' before and it doesn't last." When therapists insist on continuing in this vein, it jeopardizes the client-therapist relationship. At best, clients comment, "I feel like you do not understand the situation." At worst, they do not return.

When pursuing exceptions, solutions and problem-free futures feels like swimming upstream, change directions and either become problem-focused, as described previously, or become pessimistic and observe what follows.

Recently Michele was working with a couple who came for marital therapy. For 40 minutes she grilled them about the strengths in their relationship. They were not particularly helpful in supplying her with information. He had considered leaving, but hadn't, and although she claimed she did not want him to leave, she could not explain which parts of the relationship were, in her opinion, worthy of salvation.

Finally, Michele switched gears. She asked him what prevented them from splitting. He said they both loved their eighteen-month-old child. The wife said that, no matter what, she still loved him. Michele then played "devil's advocate" for a while. They appeared a bit surprised. The tone in the session changed at that point.

At the end of the session Michele told them that, based on what she heard from them, she was unclear as to why they wanted to maintain their marriage. She indicated that they must know something about their relationship that she did not. They were asked to "notice what is happening that is evidence that they should stay together."

They returned with extensive lists of things that went well between them. They were smiling and affectionate. The woman later told Michele that she knew what was for her the turning point. She said, "When you said to us last session, 'Why don't you just separate?' it really scared us. We knew we had to get our act together." Knowing when to shift gears is a real skill in doing therapy.

A DAY IN SCHOOL: A CASE STUDY

The following case depicts a first session almost in its entirety, illustrating many first-session techniques. By reviewing the transcript, readers will get a glimpse of how the techniques are woven together to produce an interview which is, itself, an intervention.

Session 1

Present are the therapist (Michele), stepmother Barb, father, and son, Jason. Jason left his biological mother's home and moved into his father's home approximately three weeks before the first session. His poor school performance was the reason for the move.

MICHELE   Okay, without any further ado . . .

BARB   (To Jason) Sorry, now you gotta talk.

MICHELE   Or at least listen. [Suggesting that therapeutic success is not contingent on the boy's talking] (Barb laughs.)

MICHELE   So, what brings you in?

BARB   Well, we want to somehow, we want to get Jason, I don't know if it's to like school, we've got to keep Jason in school. Mr. Dean [assistant dean] says when Jason wants to leave school, Jason walks out the door and leaves school and he says that's the only real problem he has with him. So we want Jason to be in school. He may not like school, but learn to live with it a little better. He's not passing real well right now.

MICHELE   Okay. (To Dad) What's your understanding of this situation?

DAD   Basically that. He don't . . . He has a hard time, I don't know if he doesn't understand . . . why he can't make himself understand why he has to take English which has poetry in it. You know, typical things — "Why do I have to study this? I'll never need it later." He's just become, he has the impression that none of it is ever going to do him any good, that he should get out and get a job.

MICHELE   When was the last time you were in school? [Searching for exceptions immediately.]

JASON   Today.

MICHELE   You went today? (Enthusiastically) How come? (Barb laughs.)

JASON   I had in-school suspension.

BARB   Oh, we didn't know that.

DAD   He doesn't cut everyday. He's never taken off a week or anything like that. He cuts generally a class or two and then goes back.

MICHELE   You do?

JASON   Just the class I don't like.

MICHELE   Now wait a second. You haven't just taken the whole week off?

JASON   No. The most I've ever taken off is a day.

MICHELE   Is that right?

JASON   (Nods)

MICHELE   How do you force yourself to go back? I mean, a lot of kids take off a day and they feel too uncomfortable to go back.

DAD   Yeah, that's what I asked him.

MICHELE   [Bypasses Dad's efforts to understand the problem and delves into what is working instead.] But to take off a class, how do you get yourself to go back?

JASON   If it's a class I don't want to go to I just leave and go up town and I go do something until it's time for the next class. I just go back.

*   *   *   *   *

BARB   Well, one thing Dad said, Jason does turn 16 in the fall which is driver license time. Dad said that if he can't pass school, he will not sign for his driver's license. I think that's a motivation.

MICHELE   You believe him? When your Dad says something does he stick to it?

JASON   Usually.

BARB   Oh yeah. He was positive about it. He said it's not a punishment.

MICHELE   Yeah.

BARB   What he said in the car, which I thought was great, is that if you are not mature enough to pass school, you're not mature enough to drive.

*   *   *   *   *

DAD   None of this problem is lack of intelligence. It's just lack of motivation.

BARB   That would be one thing. I mean like I said, "Jason, if you were a stupid . . ." that's just it — the kid's not stupid.

MICHELE   Obviously.

Here father attributes a cause to the problem — the boy's lack of motivation. Michele chooses to focus on the fact that the boy is intelligent and tactfully avoids a discussion of his motivation.

BARB   (Emphatically) Oh no, he's not.

DAD   According to his record he's average or better.

BARB   I say he's above average.

MICHELE   Dad, is it different for you to take a strong stand like that in regards to the car? Is that kind of different?

DAD   Yeah.

MICHELE   So, you've turned over a new leaf? [Attempting to emphasize and amplify changes]

DAD   Well, no. I think I've been kind of neglectful as far as him because if he was getting D's or C's and making it through school, none of this would have come to pass. But, his being in a failing status with everything and skipping school and running around, it shocked me into saying, "I've got to do something concrete for a change." So, I guess you could call it a new leaf.

Notice that at first Dad responds, "Well, no," to the therapist when asked whether he turned over a new leaf, but ends his speech contradicting that. His perception shifted as he produced evidence of his new behavior.

MICHELE   So, when did you come to that decision? [Michele presupposes that this new leaf was an active decision on Dad's part.]

DAD   When he started doing so badly when it was really affecting him. I figured it's time to try and do something. [Dad accepts and validates this active decision frame.]

MICHELE   How long ago was that? He's been obviously moving in this direction for some time. [Michele further crystallizes this reality by asking about it in the past tense, "How long ago *was* that?"]

DAD   Yeah. To do something this concrete was right when we told him he's going to move out with us. I've always . . . I never done it, but I always thought about it. Let's put it that way.

MICHELE   Well, okay.

DAD   I should do it, but I've been too busy with this and that. Finally, it just hit me that he's gonna flunk out of school or quit school or whatever and we gotta try and make some changes.

MICHELE   Okay. So you turned over a new leaf? (Reemphasizing)

DAD   I suppose you can say that.

*   *   *   *   *

Several minutes later, Michele shifts the session from the present to the future. Notice how there has been little discussion about the past up to this point. As Jason answers the future-oriented questions, he accepts the presupposition that he will be attending school fulltime. He is more than able to fill in all the blanks regarding what his future is to hold for him when the problem is solved.

MICHELE   Which one of your teachers will be most surprised when you are attending all the time?

JASON   Probably my history teacher.

MICHELE   Really? He's gonna be shocked?

BARB   Will they know your name? (Laughs)

MICHELE   More shocked than Mr. Dean?

JASON   Mr. Dean will be surprised that I am not in his office.

MICHELE   Yeah, I bet.

JASON   My algebra teacher will freak out.

MICHELE   Is that right?

JASON   I like math, but I do not like the teacher.

MICHELE   (Ignoring that statement) Will your history teacher be the most surprised? (Jason nods) And then your algebra teacher? (Jason nods again) Where does Mr. Dean fit into that?

JASON   I don't really know if he, cause there's kids in his office all the time, I don't know if he will notice for a while.

MICHELE   It will take him a while.

BARB   Yeah, but when I went in there I said, "Hi, my name is Barb Smith, my son . . . ," and he said, "Jason."

JASON   Oh, he knows who I am. I'll be walking down the hall and he'll say, "Hi, Jason!" all the time.

MICHELE   Okay, he's going to miss you. (Barb laughs.)

JASON   (Smiling) Probably. Because I'm in his office . . .

MICHELE   Are you going to drop in his office and say hi?

JASON   Probably not.

MICHELE   You don't like him that much? Right? . . . Who else will be surprised in school that you are attending fulltime?

JASON   I don't know, I'm sure some of the kids will wonder what's going on.

MICHELE   They are going to ask you, don't you think?

JASON   Yeah.

MICHELE   What kind of a response are you going to give them?

JASON   I'll probably tell them that I got in too deep.

MICHELE   Will they give you a hard time about that?

JASON   They'll just kid around, but they won't give me a hard time.

MICHELE   Okay . . . ah, do you think your Mom will be surprised?

JASON   Yeah.

MICHELE   What do you think she will think about it?

JASON   She'll think it's good. She'll like it a lot.

MICHELE   Okay. You know, once you have been in school for

a while and things continue to be on the right track, how's your life going to be different?

Notice "continue" to be on the right track, indicating that things are already moving in that direction. This question further crystallizes the new reality of school attendance by asking about concomitant changes in the rest of the boy's life once the school attendance is regular.

JASON   . . . I probably won't go out and party as much.

MICHELE   Okay.

JASON   I'll probably calm down a lot. When we go to birth-day parties I don't want to talk, I just kind of sit there.

MICHELE   You mean family stuff?

BARB   Yeah.

MICHELE   Are you going to be different there?

JASON   Probably.

MICHELE   How so?

JASON   Um. We don't go there very much and I don't see them very much so I kind of get nervous . . . and I guess in a way I am kind of different because my cousins are good in school and don't get into trouble a lot. Then there's me. I get into trouble all the time and I just get nervous, like they think I'm crazy or something.

MICHELE   So, once they start hearing about the fact that you're in school fulltime, you'll feel more comfortable being with them?

JASON   Probably.

MICHELE   Who is likely to tell them that you are doing okay in school?

JASON   I don't know, they seem to find out.

MICHELE   They do? Who do you think is going to tell them?

JASON   I don't know.

MICHELE   You think it will be, is it more likely to be Barb or your Dad or . . .

JASON   Probably Barb. (Barb laughs.)

MICHELE   It will be Barb? She's going to brag about you, huh? . . . Who will she tell first?

JASON   Hopefully my uncle.

BARB   Oh, that's true. I was going to say Grandma, but that's true.

MICHELE   Yeah? Your uncle, why's that?

JASON   Because he is always giving me a hard time.

MICHELE   Then he'll be more shocked than Mr. Dean and all those other guys put together.

JASON   Probably.

MICHELE   I am going to take a break and talk to my team members and see what they have to say and then I'll give you some feedback.

*   *   *   *   *

MICHELE   (returning from break) We are impressed that you decided to resolve the situation once and for all. For example, by your having Jason move into your home so that you could provide more structure, by your deciding that there needed to be consequences if there continues to be a problem, like the driver's license, and also by your deciding to — both of you — be firmer and spend more time with Jason. Those are all fairly strong actions to resolve this thing once and for all. And Barb, the team is very impressed with all of your interest in Jason and your enthusiasm even though Jason isn't really your . . .

Notice that the message says "if" there continues to be a problem, creating a doubt that the problem will happen but still recognizing that possibility.

BARB   Oh, that has never really mattered to me if Jason is really mine or not.

MICHELE   I know. In some families it does matter and so we
     are impressed with that. And you hardly seem like the
     "wicked step-mother." (A description she gave of herself
     earlier in the session)

BARB   (Laughs) I can be, be honest.

DAD   She has her days.

BARB   "Bitch" and me get along good on some days.

MICHELE   Okay. In any case, we are impressed with the ob-
     vious caring for Jason.

BARB   I do, a lot.

MICHELE   And Jason, we're impressed that you do go to
     school everyday and that you do attend classes and you
     do have some definite plans to buckle down and attend
     classes until school is out. (To parents) We want to pre-
     dict for you that there may be some rough spots in
     adding a new family member to your family.

Again, the message emphasizes the positive—Jason does go
to school everyday. The team goes on to put some words in
Jason's mouth or perhaps to attribute to him a stronger position than he espoused—they tell him that they are impressed that he has definite plans to buckle down and attend
classes until school is out. Before he has time to object or
really even consider this, a message is given to the parents,
which distracts everyone and makes it less likely they will
challenge this positive attribution.

BARB   Oh yeah.

MICHELE   In fact, one of the members of the team thinks
     that there may be more than sort of rough spots, that
     things might be really rough at times.

BARB   Oh yeah.

MICHELE   In any case, I have a homework assignment for
     you to do in between now and the next time we meet to
     give me some more basic information. And that is to

notice what's happening around your home, or in other aspects of your life too if you want, notice what's happening that you would like to continue to have happen, okay? You got that? (Jason nods.) (To Jason) I hope this is the kind of homework you do. (Barb laughs.)

This is the "first session task" developed at BFTC. Michele also injects some humor into the situation by calling this homework and then joking with the boy about doing it.

Session 2 — Stepmother and Jason Present

MICHELE   What was happening that you'd like to continue to happen?

BARB   He was great! You couldn't ask for a better kid this week. I mean, he's done nothing wrong.

MICHELE   You're kidding?

BARB   No skipping school, nothing.

MICHELE   Now wait a second. (Barb laughs.) Wait a minute. (Jokingly)

BARB   I know, I know, I know.

MICHELE   You've been to every class?

JASON   Except study hall.

MICHELE   Is that right? (Impressed)

BARB   The only thing he did is he screwed up his ankle this week and he's on crutches. But he couldn't help that.

MICHELE   Now wait a second, wait a second.

BARB   I mean he's done nothing. He comes right home after school.

MICHELE   How'd you get that to happen?

BARB   (Laughs) I'm not kidding, you couldn't ask for a better kid this week.

MICHELE   You haven't gotten into trouble? You haven't been called to Mr. Dean's office?

JASON   Nope.

MICHELE   What's going on?

BARB   I went up yesterday to pay for his driver's education and we told him to take driver's education you have to take another course to make up, fine, he never said anything more. So I went up there to check on his attendance and she goes, "Well let me see." Well, you see he was in detention last week. He had to be in one class all week to make up for mistakes from before. So, she checked on Monday and she goes, "No, he didn't skip." She checked on Tuesday, she said, "No, he didn't skip." So today I said, "I didn't call up, did you skip at all today?" and he said, "No, I didn't skip." . . . He's even bringing his . . . books home! (Laughter) I know.

MICHELE   Wait a minute. You've been in detention last week, but this week you're back to regular classes? Even classes you didn't like? (Jason nods.) What's that like?

JASON   Pretty boring. (Barb laughs.)

MICHELE   I know that. Gosh, I don't even know what to say.

JASON   Neither did the teachers.

Jason noticed the teachers' shocked reactions. The future-oriented question in the previous session—"Which of your teachers will be most surprised?"—probably influenced him.

MICHELE   Now . . .

BARB   He's really great at home. Clean bedroom.

MICHELE   Is that different?

BARB   Yeah, at his house I know it was never clean. His sister used to tell me that it was disastrous. He's been great!

MICHELE   I'm like speechless.

BARB   We've been speechless!

Session 3

Several of Jason's teachers told him that even if he were to attend their classes for the remainder of the school year he would not receive a passing grade. Jason decided to cut those classes although he attended all others. When Mr. Dean discovered that Jason had been cutting again he was very angry, but was willing to work out an arrangement with Jason. He told Jason that he could drop the courses he was failing if he promised to attend the other classes consistently until school was out. Jason agreed.

Session 4

Jason stuck to his bargain and finished out the school year without any further cutting. We ended our sessions and left open the option of resuming if necessary in the fall. No further contact was made.

6.

Prescriptions for Change
Altering the Doing and
the Viewing of the Problem

In solution-oriented therapy we are trying to do three things:

1. *Change the "doing" of the situation that is perceived as problematic.* We want to change the actions and interactions involved in the situation, freeing clients to use other, atypical actions that are more likely to resolve their situations than repeating unsuccessful patterns. A change in what they do can also bring about a change in their frame of reference. In addition, changes in the "doing" of the situation can elicit new or forgotten strengths and abilities.

2. *Change the "viewing" of the situation that is perceived as problematic.* Changing clients' frames of reference both in the session and outside the therapy room can lead to changes in action and the stimulation of unused potentials and resources.

3. *Evoke resources, solutions and strengths to bring to the situation that is perceived as problematic.* Reminding people of their resources and bringing forth those

strengths and abilities can lead to changes in actions and viewpoint.

In this chapter, we take up three aspects of solution-oriented therapy that are designed to accomplish these three tasks.

PATTERN INTERVENTION:
THE BUTTERFLY EFFECT

In a recent book on an emerging paradigm in the physical sciences (Gleick, 1987), several ideas emerge that neatly summarize the ideas involved in pattern intervention. Scientists studying chaotic and complex situations have begun to discover some new ways of viewing these phenomena. The first is the discovery that seemingly random and complex situations have underlying organizing patterns. Even those events that are very regular, like heartbeats, have chaotic variations that also have underlying patterns.

We enter a world where "things" are really constantly changing and varying, with underlying patterns organizing them into their "thinglike" appearance. Chaos is surprisingly orderly. These chaotic systems are also surprisingly changeable. When perturbed, they respond by rearranging their patterns. This effect was first noted by meteorologist Edward Lorenz, who was using a computer to analyze the effects a small change would have on global weather patterns. What he found was that the most minute changes have a profound effect on complex systems like weather. This effect was dubbed the "Butterfly Effect," because, as Lorenz put it, if a butterfly flapped its wings in Brazil, it might produce a tornado in Texas. Lorenz found that when he had a computer graphically represent these patterns of chaos, there were points of order—"strange attractors"—that organized the chaos into beautiful shapes and patterns.

In therapy we seek to alter the "strange attractors" of individual and social patterns by introducing a small change into them. We find the points of order in the seeming chaos of the client's presenting situation and systematically perturb those pattern organizers. Freud had a dictum, "Where id was, ego shall be." We would restate that, "Where rigid patterns were, flexibility shall be."

In earlier chapters, we discussed the idea that the problems people bring to therapy are not things at all, but patterns of constantly changing talk, thought and action. These patterns are very susceptible to change. The situations or contexts in which these patterns are contained are part of the pattern. In the following pages, we describe ways to intervene in the patterns that make up the complaint in order to change those contexts so they no longer contain problems or "symptoms" (O'Hanlon, 1982a, 1987; O'Hanlon and Wilk, 1987).

Complaint Pattern Intervention

Frequently the easiest and most straightforward way to intervene in a context containing a complaint is to alter the pattern of the complaint itself (what we mean by complaint here is what therapists commonly call a "symptom," a term we avoid because it implies that what someone complains about is the manifestation of some underlying pathology). The therapist arranges for the client(s) to alter the performance of the complaint in some small or insignificant way. The work of Milton Erickson contains many examples of this type of intervention. Erickson might direct a compulsive handwasher to change the brand of soap he uses to wash his hands. Or he might get a person who smokes to put her cigarettes in the attic and her matches in the basement. He told a thumbsucker to suck her thumb for a set period of time every day. He directed a couple who argued about who was to drive home after a party (at which they'd both had a few drinks) that one was to drive from the party to one block before home; then they were to stop the car, switch places and the other was to drive the rest of the way home (Rossi, 1980; Haley, 1973).

Altering the performance of the complaint alters the context. Often the complaint disappears, either gradually or abruptly.

A client who compulsively pulled out her hair (in medical jargon, this is called trichotillomania) was told that every day she pulled hair from the usual place (a patch directly above her forehead), she would have to pull out one hair from the back of her head. She found that she had less inclination to compulsively pull out the hair in front when she knew she would have to deliberately pull another out. Next, she was given the burdensome task of having to wrap each hair that she pulled out of her head very tightly around a matchstick. This turned out to be a very significant change because she had also, unbeknownst to the therapist, felt a compulsion to pull off the root of each hair she pulled out of her head — that was part of her ritual. She found she was unable to wrap the hair around the matchstick without the bulk of the root. She began pulling her hair out only infrequently. As her hair started to grow back, she took much more interest in her appearance. She got a new hairstyle and rather long artificial nails. Finding that the length of the artificial nails prevented her from pulling out her hair, she finally stopped completely.

The classes of interventions that can be used in this realm are summarized in the list below, with an example provided to illustrate each type of pattern intervention:

1. Change the frequency or rate of the performance of the complaint.

   A client who usually ate sweets very frantically during binges was told to deliberately eat candy slowly when not on a binge.

2. Change the timing of performance of the complaint.

   A depressed client was told to schedule her depression for a certain time each night, rather than waiting for it to occur randomly.

3. Change the duration of the performance of the complaint.

   A "compulsive" handwasher might be told to wash his left hand for at least five minutes and his right hand for no longer than 30 seconds at each handwashing.

4. Change the location of the performance of the complaint.

   A student of Bill's was doing therapy with a couple who complained of having unproductive and quite vicious arguments which both would later regret. He and they had tried many ways to resolve this situation to no avail. After learning about pattern intervention, he told the partners that the next time they started to have one of their arguments they were to retire immediately to the bathroom. Once there, the husband was to take off all his clothes and lie down in the bathtub. The wife was to sit (fully clothed) on the toilet. If they could, they were then to continue the argument. They couldn't. They began to laugh at the absurdity of the situation. After a time, when a discussion was starting to heat up, one of them would glance towards the bathroom they would both start laughing and avoid an argument.

5. Add (at least) one new element to the complaint pattern.

A client who binged was told to put on her favorite shoes before she binged. This was sufficient to interrupt the pattern and stop her bingeing.

6. Change the sequence of elements/events in the complaint pattern.

    A teenager who was tired of hearing her father's lectures about her misbehavior was told to tape record them and, when the appropriate time came, to beat her father to the punch by playing the lecture back on a tape player.

7. Break the complaint pattern into smaller pieces or elements.

    Spouses were told that they could argue only on paper. He was to have five minutes to write out his side of the argument; then he was to pass the paper to the other person so she could write her piece of the argument.

8. Link the complaint performance to the performance of some burdensome activity.

    A couple on the verge of divorce consulted Bill for therapy. The husband was, they both agreed, a "workaholic," who constantly broke his word about being home early in the evening from his job. When he would arrive home from his 9 to 5 job at 8:30 or 9:00 p.m., his wife would invariably greet him with harsh words and a fight would ensue. He began arriving home even later and later, in the hopes that she would be asleep and that he could avoid their nightly argument. His only day off was Sunday, which he typically spent asleep or watching TV in a recliner in the living room. She complained that this was not the kind of companion she wanted in a husband. On Sundays, she preferred to visit the homes of her parents and/or his parents. He usually complained about that and

tried his best to remain in his easy chair. He admit-
ted that he could reasonably get himself home by
8:00 p.m., no matter what came up at work. It was
agreed that she would no longer say a word to him
about being late when he arrived home from work.
However, she was to keep track of how many min-
utes after 8:00 p.m. he arrived. At the end of the
week, she was to tally the time and he was to
spend that amount of time visiting the relatives
that Sunday without griping. He soon became
very punctual in arriving home.

Context Pattern Intervention

When pattern intervention with the complaint does not
work or is inadvisable, you can alter the personal or interpersonal patterns surrounding or accompanying the complaint.
This type of intervention consists of altering patterns that
do not directly involve the performance of the complaint.
For example, a person who binges on food may avoid going
out with friends on the days when she has been bingeing.
Although not socializing with friends does not directly involve bingeing, it is an accompanying pattern that can be
altered with task assignments. She might be told that on
days when she thinks she is going to binge, she should make
a point of going out with friends. Another "binger" might
never get dressed on days when she binges. She might be
told that if she feels like bingeing, she must first get dressed
in her best looking outfit, put on her makeup and fix her
hair, then to binge if she still feels the need. Although these
accompanying regular patterns are not directly involved in
the performance of the complaint, altering them can bring
about a change in the complaint context, leading to resolution of the presenting complaint. The therapist should ask
for descriptions of actions and interactions not directly in-

volved in the complaint performance and alter those that seem to be regular accompaniments to the complaint.

Individual and interpersonal approaches are often viewed as being at odds with one another. One is either a "systemic" therapist or an "individual, linear" therapist. This approach, however, finds no conflict between the two. The unifying concept of pattern is used to bridge the (alleged) gap. What the two approaches have in common is the discovery and alteration of patterns of action surrounding the complaint. If causal, functional, and other explanatory hypotheses are avoided, no conflict need arise. How and why the patterns came to be, what function or meaning they have, and other such speculations are viewed as irrelevant and distracting to the main task: that of discerning the patterns of action and interaction surrounding the complaint and altering them. This includes such things as who is around when the complaint is performed and what others (those not directly involved in the performance) say or do about the complaint with the person or persons directly involved.

In the case below, a pattern intervention was given to an individual, but it had an interpersonal effect. The intervention changed the contextual pattern, thereby eliminating the complaint.

The woman appeared in Bill's office and said that she needed some help because she hated her daughter. As her mother described her, the girl sounded like a demon. There were two other children with whom mother got along very well, one younger than the "problem child" and one older. The girl's father saw nothing wrong with the girl. Mother, however, reported that when father wasn't home the girl would give her the most hateful looks and fight her on every little thing. She had come to hate the girl and felt very guilty about it. She wanted to know if Bill thought he could do anything to help change her feelings about the girl or to reform the girl. She was reluctant to bring the girl in to see Bill because both her husband and the girl thought there was no problem. Bill told her to record the daughter on an audio tape recorder, especially during their struggles in the morning, when mother was trying to get the children off to school and father was not around. Due to the Christmas season, a session was scheduled one month later. Mother was to bring the tape for Bill to review so he could give her some consultation.

When she returned a month later, mother had very little of interest on the tape. She said that she had been so busy with the Christmas activities for a few weeks that she had not had a chance to buy any blank tapes to make the recording. Finally, one day when her daughter was being particularly hateful, she decided that she would just go ahead and record over an old tape. When she got out the tape recorder and turned it on, the daughter noticed it and asked what it was for. When her mother explained that it was for a counselor she was seeing, the daughter refused to talk. Mother was a bit frustrated at first, but then recognized the blessing in disguise. She started turning on the tape recorder every time the daughter was giving her trouble and the trouble immediately ceased.

Bill expressed his amusement at the situation, but said he would need a tape of the daughter being hateful if he was going to be a consultant to her. Another session was scheduled for the next month. Of course, mother again appeared with an uninteresting tape. She guiltily confessed that she had occasionally turned on the tape recorder even when she had already run out of blank tape, just to stop her daughter from acting up. The month had been trouble-free and she and her daughter were starting to get closer.

After a brief discussion, she was sent on her way with solemn instructions to get Bill something juicy on the next month's tape. When mother appeared with no juicy material on the next month's tape, Bill discussed the futility of their *efforts and both he and mother agreed that the situation had improved so much that further consultation was unnecessary. Mother said that she had realized during the past month that she may have been part of the problem, because in listening to the tapes she made, she noticed that she always spoke more considerately to her daughter when the tape recorder was on since she knew Bill would be listening to it. Bill agreed that it usually takes two to tango, but dismissed all that as irrelevant speculation now that the problem was gone.*

SOLUTION PRESCRIPTIONS:
FORMULAS FOR CHANGE

One particularly interesting aspect of the work of the BFTC and Milan teams is the development of particular interventions which seem to be effective in resolving extremely varied kinds of presenting problems. In other words, the same task is utilized to initiate changes in such problems as bed-wetting, school phobia, or marital difficulties. The BFTC team calls these interventions "formula tasks," while "invariant prescription" refers to a formula task developed by the team in Milan. What we find so intriguing is not necessarily the tasks themselves, but the notion that the therapist need not know a great deal about the dynamics of the difficulties to help resolve them. The specifics of the problem pattern appear to be unrelated to the solution process.

Below we describe several formula interventions which we have found useful over the years. Although invariant tasks can be either problem-oriented, i.e., designed to interrupt the complaint sequence pattern, or solution-oriented, i.e., designed to build on pre-existing solutions and strengths, the solution prescriptions described here prompt new behaviors and perceptions by creating the expectation of change in the future. They are designed to orient the attention of clients in the direction of solutions. This is a change in the "viewing" of the situation.

First Session Formula Task

> "Between now and the next time we meet, we [I] would like you to observe, so that you can describe to us [me] next time, what happens in your [*pick one*: family, life, marriage, relationship] that you want to continue to have happen." (de Shazer, 1985, p. 137)

This task, which was described in Chapter 1, was developed at BFTC and has proven useful with individuals, couples, and families alike. At one time the BFTC team used the intervention at the end of the first session in many of their cases, hence the name.

There are several interesting aspects to this task. As we have mentioned before, clients do not expect the therapist to ask about what is working, so they are sometimes surprised by the request. With this assignment, they go home wearing their looking-for-good-things glasses and, much to their surprise, they typically discover quite a few things they want to continue to have happen. Perhaps some of these worthwhile things were happening but simply went unnoticed before the task directed clients' attention to the right places.

The other interesting aspect about the way clients respond to this task is that, although the assignment does not request that they do something new or different, clients usually do just that—"turn over new leaves" and alter their behavior. When this intervention is given to a member of a couple or family, other family members notice the changes (they are also wearing looking-for-good-things glasses) and respond by changing too.

Clinically, what is most exciting about these new and different behaviors is that they generally are precisely the changes needed to solve the problem. Notice that clients are not instructed to alter anything, let alone given specific information about how to solve the problem. Somehow, they know exactly what they need to do without this guidance. We suspect that the information about exceptions, solutions, and strengths that emerges during solution-oriented sessions offers clients all the necessary data to utilize the first session task in a most productive way.

When clients return for the second session, they are asked, "So, what is happening that you would like to continue to have happen?" The solution language in both the intervention and the follow-up question indicates that the therapist is certain that good things happen and that they have been noticed. Once the good things are described, the therapist asks the series of presuppositional questions to elicit information about exceptions (see Chapter 5). This serves to amplify and maintain the changes.

THE SURPRISE TASK—
FOR COUPLES OR FAMILIES

> "Do at least one or two things that will surprise your parents [spouse, if doing marital therapy]. Don't tell them what it is. Parents, your job is to see if you can tell what it is that she is doing. Don't compare notes; we will do that next session."

This task introduces a bit of randomness into the patterns that characterize relationships; things become more unpredictable. Again, as in the first session task, clients are keeping their eyes open for new behaviors. Those who are trying on new behaviors needn't worry that their deeds will go unnoticed.

There is a playfulness about this task. Across the board,

when clients are instructed to do the surprise task, they immediately smile. It changes the context of their difficulties. What may have been a battle or a war for months or years now takes on a "game-like" quality. (Solving problems can be fun.) If clients exhibit a sense of humor during the session, success with this task is almost guaranteed.

When clients return, rather than asking person A what he did to surprise the others, we ask person B, "What did you notice person A doing this week?" and vice versa. Generally, more than two surprises are reported, and sometimes person A is given credit for doing something he did not intentionally mean to do "as the surprise." Sometimes person A will silently take credit for that surprise and no one is the wiser. Laughter usually surfaces as notes are compared. Most importantly, the particular "surprises" that were implemented usually develop into solutions.

The Generic Task

Once clients have described what their goal might be, even if they have had difficulty being specific, it is possible to use their language to design an intervention which creates the expectancy for change. For example, if a client wants "more peace of mind," suggest, "Keep track of what you are doing this week that gives you more peace of mind." Or, if a client wants "to feel more in control of my life," suggest, "Keep track of what you are doing this week that makes you feel more in control of things." We may suggest that clients write down their observations, or we may simply suggest that they return prepared to tell us about their findings. Obviously, this task presupposes that desirable behaviors will occur in between therapy sessions — and they usually do. An added benefit of this task is that vague clients return having defined their goals more clearly.

SOLUTION-ORIENTED HYPNOSIS

Most people, including therapists, have an image of hypnosis that is derived from the portrayal of traditional hypnosis in the popular media. The powerful, charismatic hypnotist with the swaying watch or the compelling eyes puts his subject "under" and programs them to do or think something.

We want to provide another image of hypnosis here, one that is based on the work of Milton Erickson and suited to a solution orientation. Much of solution-oriented therapy evolved from Erickson, who used hypnosis in many of his cases. Some of his work with hypnosis was uncovering work directed towards finding the "unconscious" meaning, function, or origin of the problem, but much of it was oriented directly towards solutions. It has become popular in Ericksonian circles to use the phrase "accessing unconscious resources."

We have already mentioned one of Erickson's hypnotic techniques, "pseudo-orientation in time," which was clearly a forerunner of solution-oriented work. In addition, Erickson blurred the boundaries between nonhypnotic and hypnotic therapy. He developed a "naturalistic" trance technique that involved no obvious trance induction ritual. At times, he did not even tell the client he was using hypnosis. This is important for our work in solution-oriented therapy, because it indicates that hypnotic "suggestions" do not require the ritual of trance induction to have an effect.

In solution-oriented hypnosis, we are concerned with awakening abilities that the subject already has but has not used in the problem context. In nonhypnotic solution-oriented therapy, the focus is upon views or actions that clients can consciously use to achieve their goals, whereas in solution-oriented hypnosis the concern is with automatic experiences, actions beyond the person's deliberate control. For example, if outside of trance you were asked to make some part of your body become numb, you would not usually be able to make that happen deliberately. In hypnosis, for some reason, many people can make parts of their bodies numb. This is what we call an involuntary skill. Hypnosis is very useful for arousing those kinds of abilities that are beyond one's conscious, deliberate control.

How are these skills evoked? One way is to just talk about experiences that are in the class of solutions to be evoked. For example, if the class of solutions that would help the person in pain is "relaxation," the therapist could talk about a time when the client soaked in a hot bath and felt very relaxed afterwards; a vacation might be mentioned, or a backrub. Another way is to give a permissive suggestion that the person has the ability to relax. This is different from traditional authoritarian hypnotic suggestion, which usually tells the subject that he or she *will* relax or *is* relaxed. In this solution-oriented approach, the client is told that he or she *can* relax. This often bypasses any "resistance" and allows the client to find his or her own means of solving the problem. The therapist merely gives a suggestion (as one of our colleagues is fond of saying, "I'm only a hypnotist, so this is only a suggestion!"); it is up to the client whether or not to take the suggestion.

The man who was seeking therapy for cluster headaches described them by saying that they are like migraines, except that they come in groups. A phase might last days, weeks, or months, with one severe headache following another. The victim never knew how long they would last. "They call 'em .45 caliber headaches," he said with a finger to his temple, "'cause when you have one you want to blow your brains out." Having suffered from them for many years, he had finally exhausted his medical options. After sending him to a number of specialists, his doctor had told him that he had nothing more medically to offer him. His daughter, having heard about Bill's use of hypnosis for headaches, encouraged her father to seek his help, although he was most skeptical about hypnosis.

After inducing a trance (although the man was never convinced that he went into a trance in either of the sessions in this treatment), Bill told the man that he knew several things about his headaches that he did not know he knew. One was that he already knew very well how to eliminate his headaches. He knew this because he had had so many headaches and somehow made them go away. His body, Bill continued, knew exactly how to create a headache and how to eliminate one. Since he was an expert at eliminating severe headaches, having had so much experience with them, he could use this "unconscious knowledge" (since he certainly had no conscious idea of how he did this) to immediately eliminate the headaches should another one ever start.

He knew another thing that he did not consciously know, as well, Bill told him. He knew the patterns of his headaches. He had reported that they always started with an intense sensation in one point in his face. Then that point of sensation would spread into a full blown headache. Bill told him that his unconscious mind could change that pattern in any way that would break him out of the headache rut.

Bill told the man that he had all these abilities and more, but there was no way to determine which ones would be most useful, how quickly he could find relief, or whether the relief would be total or only partial. At the end of the first session, he was unconvinced of the value of this approach and was sure that he was not in trance. He returned only at the urging of his wife and daughter, who convinced him that one session was not enough to find out whether it would work. At the second session, he was again convinced he had fallen asleep and not been in a trance at all. After that session, though, he had an important experience: He left the office with the beginnings of a headache and as he had sat behind the wheel of his car in the parking lot, the intense

*spot of sensation that usually led into a headache just dissi-
pated and drained out of his face. When the same thing
happened the next day, he knew that the headaches had
been eliminated. The client returned for a one session
"booster shot" two years later when he felt the headaches
coming on again. Follow-up indicates that he remains free of
cluster headaches three years later.*

Another use for solution-oriented hypnosis is to aid in the
recall of experiences that can serve as references for building
the skills necessary to solve the presenting difficulty. Again,
this contrasts with traditional uses of hypnosis, in which
clients are encouraged to recall traumatic memories and
work them through.

*The young woman had been through the gamut of medi-
cal and psychological tests and treatments, but was still unable to achieve orgasm. In trance, Bill suggested that she
may have at one time had an orgasm, but may have been
unaware that she had, due to her lack of experience in the
area. She replied without hesitation that she now remembered that she had had an orgasm during her sleep one
night. (When she had been asked the same question out of
trance, she had reported never having had an orgasm.) After
she remembered the nighttime orgasm in trance, she became convinced that having orgasms was possible for her,
which eventually led to her having orgasms regularly, first
through masturbation, then with a partner.*

Sometimes, when therapy is at an impasse, we induce a
trance and ask the client what needs to be done to make
progress or resolve the presenting problem. Many times, clients who were not able to give any conscious help are able
during trance to clearly tell us how to help them. These
experiences have reinforced for us the idea that clients are
the experts regarding how to solve their problems. Neverthe-

less, the therapist must have the skill to create a context that will elicit clients' expertise and help them use it in their lives. In this case, the therapist's expertise involves creating a context for solution-oriented trance.

As in our nonhypnotic work, we make much use of presupposition in solution-oriented hypnosis. Erickson had a favorite form of presupposition that he called the "illusion of alternatives." This technique involves giving the client a choice between several alternatives, each of which will result in success.

Erickson treated a 12-year-old boy who wet the bed. Erickson first oriented him to the future by talking about how big and tall he would be when he was a man. Would he be taller or larger than his father?, Erickson wondered aloud. The boy got involved in this image and, as he did, Erickson launched into a monologue that turned into a naturalistic trance induction. He told the boy that this was Monday and did he think he could have a permanent dry bed by the next night? Erickson didn't think so, he said, the boy didn't think so and anyone with any brains didn't think so. Did he think he could have a permanent dry bed by Wednesday? Again, Erickson doubted it very much. In fact, he didn't think the boy would have a dry bed that week. He also expected it to be wet next Monday, Erickson said, but he was puzzled by one thing. Would the boy have a dry bed by accident next Wednesday or would it be next Thursday? The boy would have to wait until next Friday morning to find out. The boy was instructed to report back the next Friday afternoon on which day it had been. When the boy returned the next week, he gleefully told Erickson he had been mistaken. It wasn't either Wednesday or Thursday — it was both.

Erickson replied that just having two dry beds in succession was not having permanent dry beds. Again, Erickson wondered aloud whether, since this was the middle of January, the boy would be able to learn to have permanent dry beds by the end of the month. Erickson supposed he couldn't learn it that fast and reminded the boy that February was a short month. He didn't know whether the boy would begin having his permanent dry bed on March 17th, which was St. Patrick's Day, or on April Fool's Day (April 1st). The boy didn't know either, Erickson said, but one thing he was sure of, Erickson emphasized, was that it was none of his business, nor would it ever be any of his business, when the boy's permanent dry beds began. (Rossi, 1980, Vol. 1, pp. 416–417)

Erickson commented that he wanted to reorient the boy. "I didn't want him thinking about a wet bed. I wanted him thinking about the remote future and the things he could do instead of thinking: what am I going to do tonight — wet the bed" (p. 417).

This case illustrates Erickson's future orientation and his use of presupposition and expectancy to create solutions. He gave the boy the illusion of alternatives between Wednesday and Thursday and between March 17th and April 1st. He oriented the boy towards the goal by focusing his thinking on *dry* beds and when he would have *permanent* dry beds. He also thrust the responsibility back to the boy and his resources when he told the boy that it would never be any of his business when the boy began to have permanent dry beds.

The purpose of solution-oriented hypnosis is not to help clients get insight into repressed memories or relive traumatic events or to program clients with new, more positive beliefs. Instead its purpose is to stimulate and use nonconsciously mediated processes, memories, and experiences to resolve clients' complaints and to create the expectancy of change.

7.

Amplifying and Maintaining Change
Keeping the Ball Rolling

Commonly, therapists ask us, "I seem to be skillful in help-ing to initiate change, but then things reach a plateau or even start to backslide. What do you do to keep change going?"

RESPONDING TO CLIENTS' RESPONSES: THE SECOND AND SUBSEQUENT SESSIONS

We typically begin our second and subsequent sessions checking into the results of the homework. Our opening question is a carefully worded presuppositional question: "So, what was happening that you wanted to continue to have happen?" or "What did you notice that you were doing that gave you more self-confidence?" or "What good things have you been doing this week?" We do *not* ask: "Did you do the homework?" or "How did the homework go?" or "Did you notice any good things that happened this week?" As with all presuppositional questions, our opening question expresses our certainty that they did the task and that good things happened; in addition, it is specific rather than vague. More specific questions channel clients in more productive directions.

Once clients respond to our opening question with any positive response we ask the series of exception questions described in Chapter 5. This amplifies the changes. We use the past tense as we investigate the differences between the good things that happened in between session one and two and the times in the past when the problem used to happen: "How did you get that to happen?" "How did it make your day go differently?" "Who else noticed that things went smoothly?" And so on.

We talk about the changes and the positive aspects of the changes as long as possible. When working with couples or families, it is fairly easy to keep this discussion going for most of the session since everyone is asked how the positive changes have had an impact on his or her life.

At the risk of oversimplifying, let us categorize clients as falling into one of three groups in terms of the amount of change experienced between session one and two. There are those who return reporting a miraculous week — a "one-session cure." Everything was perfect, far beyond their wildest dreams. This we call the "miracle group." The second category is the "so-so group." They had a better week than weeks previous, but there was still evidence that the problem is not completely resolved yet. The third group reports no changes or perhaps regression. This group we call "same or worse."

The structure of second and subsequent sessions depends on the amount of change clients report in between sessions. What follows is a "decision tree" to guide clinicians in amplifying and maintaining the changes their clients have initiated.

The Miracle Group

As we discussed at the beginning of this section, we encourage clients to talk about change in as much detail and for as long as possible. If miracles have occurred between sessions, this is an extremely easy task. Clients are pleased and eager to discuss their accomplishments. By the end of the session, both therapist and clients should have a very clear picture of what the changes are, how they occurred, and most importantly, what needs to happen in order for the changes to continue. Each person (if there is more than one client) should be asked this question: "What do you need to do to keep the changes going?" or "What does she need to do . . . ?"

Here is another important question that will increase the likelihood that changes will continue: "Is there anything that might happen in the next week or two which might present a challenge to keeping these good things going?" If they say "no," fine. If they answer "yes," ask, "What would that challenge be?" Then encourage them to describe in detail their perception of the potential difficulty. Then ask, "How will you handle it differently this time?" (Again, notice the use of the words "might," a tentative term and "will," a definitive one.) Clients usually ponder this for a while and then come up with a reasonable plan. If they have trouble thinking of a creative way to handle the situation, suggestions by the therapist are usually welcomed. So that nothing gets overlooked, it is useful to ask, "Is there anything else that might pop up which might be challenging?" Repeat this series of questions until it is felt that no stone is left unturned. Many clients comment that it helps to have a plan when difficulties arise.

Even in the miracle group there are skeptics, and rightfully so. Based on past experience many people find it necessary to shield themselves from the disappointment of things rapidly deteriorating. The fear is "easy come, easy go." These folks say, "He has followed our rules for a period of time before and then he just blows it," or "I've had several good nights' sleep in the past and then my insomnia comes back full force."

This is not "resistance" or unreasonable pessimism; rather, this is very useful information. The therapist's task now becomes uncovering the past pattern of the ups and downs. The following dialogue illustrates this process.

THERAPIST   In the past, when he was following your rules, how long a period would he usually go before he blew it?

CLIENT   Two or three weeks.

THERAPIST   Okay. So, if he were to stay on track for three and a half or four weeks would that be different?

CLIENT   Yes, it would.

THERAPIST   Then, would you have to wonder whether this time is really different? Would you start to think that perhaps this time the changes are going to stick?

CLIENT   I guess so.

The method here is to add on only a small period of time to the longest time in the past that things went well and ask if that would be a difference that makes a difference. If so, when three and a half weeks go by, it will serve as a context marker—"this means the change is going to stick." In this case, rather than "waiting for the other shoe to fall," as they have in the past, these clients can relax and expect that the changes will continue. If the therapist's time frame does not seem like enough to make a difference to the client, the client is asked to define the time limit. Naturally, this too might require a negotiation process to assure that the goal is attainable.

We do not, as a rule, predict relapses or setbacks because we worry about self-fulfilling prophecies. Furthermore, much of the time these predictions are not necessary or appropriate. However, if things have been "perfect," and for some reason it is our clinical judgment that there may be a setback, we might say, "I am concerned that since all of your days were 'perfect,' when you have a day that is just 'normal,' you might incorrectly think that things are sliding back to square one. Everyone has ups and downs, no matter how well things are going in general." This normalizes and pre-empts any potential difficulty.

At the end of a miracle session we often ask our clients whether they want to schedule another session. Occasionally they already feel satisfied with the results and require no further sessions. Most of the time though, we schedule another session for one or two weeks later. We might even call it a "check up" session. As in the first session, we comment on all changes; and we might also suggest that they continue to look for signs that these changes are sticking.

The So-so Group

After the question, "So what good things happened this week?" (or some variation), certain clients begin discussing a few of the difficulties they tangled with in that period. We politely but firmly interrupt and suggest, "Hang on. . . . We will get to that in just a minute. First, I would like to hear about the good things that happened." Redirecting the session at this juncture is valuable for a couple of reasons. First, clients generally can recall the pleasant moments during the past week and often the pleasant times vastly outweighed the unpleasant ones. This, then, changes clients' perspective of the significance of the "not-so-good" times; they seem less important by the end of the session. The talk of good times provides an excellent context in which to later discuss difficulties. Second, we want clients to know that the most direct way to solutions is to examine what is working. Clients get the message that this is the information we need to help them most efficiently.

When the analysis of strengths and solutions is completed, we might ask, "So, what were you concerned about?" We get a description of what remains of the problem and then, once again, ask about exceptions, "How did you handle it differently this time?" If there is still a problem, we follow the problem-focused track described in the previous chapter in order to design an appropriate and effective pattern intervention.

With this group, we may use the scaling question, a therapeutic tool developed at BFTC which has proven invaluable in terms of maintaining and amplifying change (Lipchik, 1988, pp. 113–114 and E. L. Rossi, personal communication). Clients are asked to rate, on a one-to-ten scale, their situations prior to coming for therapy (or whenever things weren't going well). Then they are asked to rate the last week on the same scale. Finally, they are asked where they would have to rate themselves in order to feel satisfied. The third rating question provides clients with the opportunity to recognize that things don't have to be perfect in order to be satisfactory.

So, if a client rates her life at a "2" before therapy, and a "6" last week and says she would need to be at an "8" to feel satisfied, we then ask, "What are one or two things you can do in the next week or two to bring you up to a $6^1/2$ or 7?" We want to make certain that what is identified is attainable. A useful homework assignment that resembles the formula tasks in structure and extends the scaling questions is: "In between now and the next time we meet, notice and keep track of all the '7' things you are doing."

Same or Worse Group

When clients report that things have remained the same or gotten worse, we do not accept this report at face value without further investigation. It is rather like that courtroom situation where the attorney objects because the witness is drawing conclusions. We return to the evidence; that is, we ask about what specifically happened between sessions related to the complaint and how it was handled.

After an initial consultation for a pain problem, one of Bill's clients returned for the second session reporting no change. When he was asked to describe more specifically how, what, and when he had experienced pain in the past few weeks, it turned out that there was a change in the time that the pain occurred. He had previously experienced pain consistently at night. Now it invariably happened during the mornings. Remembering that the man had complained of losing a great deal of sleep because his pain kept him awake at night, Bill asked him if he had been sleeping better. The man said he was sleeping well. Bill said that, as far as he was concerned, the man had arrived with two problems, insomnia and pain. He was now free of one-half of his problem, insomnia, and had made a significant change in the other one, pain (because the pain pattern had changed). Now all that was left to do was to continue the change until he experienced significant pain relief.

A supervisee was observing the session with the pain and insomnia client. Afterwards she told Bill that at the beginning of the session she had begun to view the therapy as very discouraging, but that as she heard Bill talk she started to see the possibilities for change in the situation and felt encouraged.

Occasionally clients insist that there is still a problem which looms large. Efforts to redirect the session are futile. When this happens we retrace our steps and ask ourselves whether we are missing some essential information.

Sometimes when we are stuck it helps to ask, "Whose

problem is this, anyway?" Anderson, Goolishian, Pulliam and Winderman (1986), who have developed an approach they called "problem-determined systems therapy," contend that the people who should be taken into consideration in therapy are those who think there is a problem with themselves or someone else. The customers for change are those who perceive there is a problem (Fisch, Weakland, and Segal, 1982). They are the ones who are motivated to see change and are typically motivated to do something to bring it about. They are also the ones who will have to be satisfied that a change has come about and/or that there is no longer a problem.

When we are not making any headway in therapy, we go back to the basic questions:

1. Who is our customer? Who is complaining about something? Who wants to see a change? Who perceives a problem?
2. What is the goal? How will we know when we have gotten there?

Sometimes we have to switch our focus midstream in the interview, when we find out the customer is not in our office. Perhaps the school counselor is our customer, as he is the one who thinks there's a problem. In that case, we might call the counselor and proceed with a solution-oriented interview. We would probably start by asking the counselor to help us by telling us how he'll know the family has benefited from therapy and should stop coming.

Sometimes we find we are working with someone who is not a customer and has no motivation to change. Or we are seeing someone who perceives no problem. Many "involuntary clients," including those referred by courts and schools, fall into this category. Solution-oriented techniques can be helpful with this group of clients, but sometimes nothing moves people who do not want to be in your office, do not want your help, and do not think they have a problem. Michele works quite a bit with school and court referred clients and finds ways of getting their cooperation and turning them into customers for change.

Another tack in approaching situations in which clients report not changing or getting worse is to think about the therapist and therapy being part of the problem rather than part of the solution. Just as individuals, couples and families repeat unhelpful patterns of thought and action, therapists and clients often develop unhelpful patterns and keep repeating those. If that is the situation, we try to change our part of the therapeutic pattern. We might do something unexpected, take a break from therapy, ask other family members to attend sessions, or change our strategy or demeanor in some way. Sometimes, when clients report that things are not changing or are getting worse, we find it is best to throw the impetus back to the clients and ask them to convince us that change is really necessary or desirable.

In our description of the first session (Chapter 5), we noted that, when clients respond negatively to our efforts to remain positive and solution-oriented, we sometimes become pessimistic in our approach. The same is true during second and subsequent sessions. Since as therapists we are part of the client system, we carefully observe how our clients respond to therapy interactions. If we say "black" and they say "white," it may also be true that, when we become pessimistic, they become more optimistic. In addition to observing patterns of interactions during the session, we notice intersession patterns. Simply stated, when clients respond to a straightforward task by doing the opposite of what has been suggested, therapists can utilize this pattern of response by giving tasks which suggest doing the opposite of what might be expected by the client (de Shazer, 1985; Haley, 1963; Rossi, 1980).

Erickson was well-known for his use of the "unperceived benefits" frame. He liked to introduce a new point of view to couples in which the man experienced impotence. He told the couple that the man had given the woman a great compliment. When the couple looked puzzled, he explained that many young men felt overwhelmed by their wives' beauty and responded in this way. While many would find this a bit too polyannaish, it appears as though his couples accepted it and were able to overcome (so to speak) this difficulty.

In general, we maintain and amplify the changes in therapy by continuing to be attuned to solutions. We listen for strengths and abilities; if they are not readily apparent, we seek them out. If they are still not forthcoming, we persist until we see or create an opening for change. If that fails, we shift our thinking and tack. As Alan Watts has written, "Problems that remain persistently insolvable should always be suspected as questions asked in the wrong way" (1966, p. 55). If we still aren't successful, we seek colleagues' ideas on how to change our thinking and strategy in the therapy. If that doesn't succeed, we or the client usually quit. As that wise philosopher W. C. Fields once observed, "If at first you don't succeed, try, try again. Then give up. There's no use being a damn fool about it!"

In the following pages we present two complete case descriptions to give the reader a sense of pulling together the elements discussed in the last three chapters.

MATTERS OF THE HEART

Session 1

Bonnie was a 55-year-old woman who called for an appointment because of panic attacks which occurred whenever her dear friend, aged 70, left town or was not available to her by phone. Actually, it was the friend who suggested that Bonnie call, since she was concerned about Bonnie's dependence in light of the fact that she "wouldn't be around forever."

As is usually the case, Michele made small talk before delving into the reason Bonnie sought treatment. During this process, although she was not asked about her family, Bonnie revealed that her father had died when she was a baby and her mother, to whom she was very close, had died about two years before the session. Bonnie prided herself on the fact that, during the last two years of her mother's life, she insisted that her mother be responsible for preparing family meals, since she believed that this task extended her mother's life by giving her a purpose for being alive. She also added that her completely healthy son, age 25, died in a freak, work-related accident. Typically, the "small talk" portion of the initial session does not contain this kind of information.

Michele then began the interview by asking, "So what brings you in?" Bonnie replied, "Every time my friend goes out of town or when I can't get in touch with her, I have a panic reaction. My heart starts beating fast and I feel bad. It's been this way for about five years, . . . but for the last year and a half I've been doing much better."

The remainder of the session was devoted to exploring what Bonnie was doing to make things "much better." She discussed several techniques she had developed over the years, including keeping busy, telling herself she was going to be okay when she felt her heart begin to race, working, and so on. Bonnie reported that all of these methods seemed to work for her.

Since the discussion about her ways of overcoming her fears occupied the majority of the session, Michele asked her why she decided to come in for the appointment. Apparently her friend was concerned that Bonnie would not be *able to take care of herself in the inevitable event of the friend's death. Bonnie admitted to being extremely fearful about this. They then explored other ways Bonnie met her needs in addition to being with her friend. Being with her husband and children, as well as being very active in community groups, satisfied many needs.*

Later in the session, when Bonnie talked about "the bad feeling inside" when her friend left town, Michele told her that she was confused and explained that her own mother worked in Europe. Every time her mother visited and then left town Michele also had "a bad feeling inside." However, Michele did not call this bad feeling "a panic reaction" instead, she called it "loneliness" or a longing for her mother. Michele questioned whether Bonnie had unwittingly gotten the two feelings confused, since she used to have panic attacks. Bonnie pondered this distinction for several moments and said, "I never thought about it that way."

At the end of the session Michele complimented Bonnie on how well she was dealing with her bad feeling, on all the methods she had developed on her own to make herself feel better. Michele also mentioned that it was not surprising that she had those bad feelings when someone she loved wasn't available, considering the experiences she had had in her life — losing her father at a very early age, her mother's recent death and the death of her healthy young son. In fact, she was extremely impressed that Bonnie was doing as well as she was under the circumstances.

Michele left Bonnie with one parting thought. She told her that Bonnie had applied the wisdom she used on her mother to her friend. Agreeing that people need a purpose in life to make life meaningful, Michele showed Bonnie how she had given purpose to her friend's life by helping her feel needed and wanted. This added a totally unexpected twist to the end of the session since Bonnie, until the session, had been feeling so dependent and helpless.

As a homework assignment, Bonnie was asked to notice what she did to overcome the temptation to call her friend or give in to the bad feeling if it occurred. She was to keep track of what she did instead. Another session was scheduled for two weeks later.

Session 2

Bonnie entered the room smiling and reported that she had little opportunity to practice since there was only one occasion when she felt uncomfortable at all. Her friend had promised she would call by a certain time and did not do so. Bonnie tried calling her but the line was busy. After waiting a half-hour Bonnie tried again; the line was still busy. She began to worry. Instead of this worry ending in "a panic attack," Bonnie did other things, as she said, "I caught myself talking to my bird and my dog. Then, I caught myself playing solitaire. That really worked, I settled right down. In the past I would have been hysterical by the end of the half-hour. I reminded myself that since it was raining something could have been wrong with the phone lines, or perhaps her son called from California."

Aside from this one incident, Bonnie had a good two weeks. She described herself as having more self-confidence in general (and gave several examples of this), having a more optimistic and positive outlook on life (she expected good things to happen), and taking things one day at a time — all new attitudes and behaviors for her. She found herself laughing quite a bit and was more relaxed than she had been in a long time. Her friends from the choir felt that the "old Bonnie" was back. Even her dear friend noticed the changes and seemed pleased.

When asked what she thought accounted for the changes, she said that she gave a lot of thought to what Michele had said about her "helping" her friend instead of vice versa. That made a big difference to her.

At the end of the session Michele told Bonnie that she was extremely impressed with all the changes and that she was pleased with how well she had handled the uncomfortable situation. Michele admitted not knowing whether or not to schedule another session, and Bonnie said that she would call if necessary. Michele suggested that Bonnie keep track in the future of what happened to convince her that the "old Bonnie" is here to stay. She agreed and added that the last session felt like 15 sessions in terms of her progress. Therefore, Michele noted that two sessions would make her feel as if she had 30 sessions. She laughed and said she felt like skipping and jumping out of the office, and she did just that!

ANNIE'S TOMORROW

Session 1

Annie, 28, walked into Michele's office holding a tissue in her hand; she had been crying in the waiting room. When asked, "What brings you here?" in a barely audible voice she tearfully responded, "My life is falling apart." She went on to explain that her boyfriend had just broken up with her and that she was handling the rejection very poorly. She said she was crying and depressed all the time. Her sentences were disjointed and she made little eye contact.

Immediately following a brief description of the problem, Michele asked her, "What is different about the times when you are handling things well?" Without hesitation she reported that she felt okay at work. Since Annie worked a fulltime job, Michele reminded her that she was doing fine for at least 40 hours of the week, a large portion of her life. Michele also commented that feeling okay for 40 hours a week is a far cry from being depressed "all the time," as she had first explained. Annie agreed.

Since Annie had identified a significant exception to the presenting problem (feeling okay 40 hours a week), Michele continued on this track. "When, in addition to work, are you handling things okay?" Annie said that the time she spent with her five-year-old son was very enjoyable and that during those times she did not have the opportunity to ruminate about her ex-boyfriend. Additionally, in the morning she was too hurried getting her son to the sitter and herself off to work to worry about the breakup.

By process of elimination it became clear that the only time Annie really felt down in the dumps was in the evening, during a two-hour period, after her son went to bed and before she went to sleep. She even admitted that at least two nights of the week she did not experience negative feelings. Some quick calculations revealed that, rather than being depressed "all the time," she was, in reality, down in the dumps only 10 hours a week. Within five minutes, her perception of her situation had been significantly altered.

Michele then asked, "What is different about the two evenings a week that you aren't thinking about Sam?" Those evenings, she said, she managed to keep herself busy, visiting a neighbor, sewing, or visiting relatives. She and Michele established that keeping busy was absolutely essential for her while she was getting her perspective back.

The next line of questioning focused on other ways she kept herself busy, "What do you do for fun?" Michele asked. She answered that she had very little fun. Being a single mother of a five-year-old son, she often felt overwhelmed with responsibility and went for long periods of time without socializing or participating in rewarding or stress-reducing activities. She commented that her family was not very *supportive in offering to babysit. She had lost contact with friends since becoming so preoccupied with the relationship with her ex-boyfriend. Furthermore, many of her old friendships revolved around drinking at bars, an activity in which Annie no longer wished to participate.*

Michele was curious and asked whether Annie had overcome a problem with drinking. Annie said that she had been in a residential treatment program the previous year and since then, except for one or two minor setbacks, had managed to maintain her sobriety. Michele used this information to highlight another of Annie's strengths, pointing out that she had not resorted to drinking during this stressful time.

Finally, Michele asked, "What will be the first sign that things are starting to be on the right track?" Annie said that rather than thinking about her ex-boyfriend during the evening, she would be thinking pleasant thoughts. She would be saying to herself, "Everything is going to work out fine."

After a break to consult with the team behind the mirror, Michele gave Annie the following message: "The team is very impressed that you got yourself here to resolve this situation once and for all. We are also impressed with all that you are accomplishing: holding a fulltime job, being a good mother, being a single mother without much support, and remaining sober through all this. We are really struck with all the changes you have been through recently: giving up old friends, breaking up with your boyfriend, and giving up alcohol. That's a lot of change in a short period of time. No wonder things seem out of control sometimes! We need some more information and we have a homework assignment for you. In between now and the next time we meet, we want you to notice and keep track of what is different about the evenings when you know that, Annie, things are going to work out fine."

Session 2

Annie walked in with an air of confidence that led Michele to believe that she had had a good week. Michele's suspicions were confirmed; Annie said that she had a "fantastic week." When asked, "So, what was different about the evenings when you knew that things are going to work out fine and what did you do to make the week fantastic?" Annie replied that she got out every night with her son and really enjoyed herself. She went next door to visit a girlfriend for dinner on two occasions. She also wandered down the street to say hello to a young man who caught her eye. This fellow was working on his car when she appeared but stopped to chat with her and her son. Annie also went to visit family members that week and found them to be supportive and fun. This was particularly surprising to her. When asked, "What do you think accounts for the difference in their behavior?" she responded, "I guess I feel better so I am more sociable with them." Her mother even offered to babysit.

Annie had also gotten out her old sewing machine and started sewing again, something she hadn't done in a long while. She had gotten along better with her son. She felt proud of the fact that her coworkers requested her help during the work day and that she was being considered for a promotion.

Because of her achievements, Annie rated her week as an "8" on a 1–10 scale and said that she felt more relaxed. Finally, she added that she did not cry a single time that week. That was the most surprising aspect of her week.

After the break, the team complimented her on all her continued changes and listed them to her. Since she was so high from all of her achievements (she had had a "fantastic week"), the team expressed concern that, should she simply have an "average" day, she might incorrectly think that she was sliding backwards to square one. She immediately provided reassurance that that was not true. Then the team told Annie that they were impressed that she knew what to do to keep things at an '8.' The task then followed from the last compliment; "Notice the things you are doing in the next two weeks that you rate as an '8'." An appointment was set for two weeks later.

Session 3

Michele began the session with, "So what are the '8' things that you have been doing in the last two weeks?" Annie said, "Everything was an '8'." She pulled out two legal sized pieces of paper with the events of the week carefully written down on them. She had spent time with friends and family, started an exercise program, enjoyed her work, and started dating the young man she met who lived on her street. Their relationship had blossomed in two weeks. Her son appeared to enjoy his company as well. She was delighted to have come out of her shell so rapidly.

During the course of the two weeks she had also weathered a real challenge to her recent progress. An uncle who lived in another state had committed suicide. Although she was upset by this, she felt good about her ability to reach out to friends and other family members for solace.

Michele asked, "Who beside you notices how well you have been doing?" Annie was quick to tell her that her boss had commented on her progress. In anticipation of our session, Annie told her boss that she thought that the therapist was going to tell her to "get lost."

After the consulting break, the team told Annie, "You are an amazing lady! All 8s!! You really have control of your life and you know exactly what to do to keep it going. We have only one other thing to tell you. . . . Get lost."

8.

The Road Not Taken
Paths to Avoid in Therapy

Most of this book has been focused on things one can do to make therapy more successful. Here we focus on what to avoid doing in therapy, some traps into which therapists we supervise commonly stumble. If the therapist stays on the road to solution, all is well. However when he or she strays off the main road therapy can go in unproductive directions, become mired in the swamp of pathology, or follow dead-end roads with no solutions in sight. We would like to put up warning signs to keep the therapist from wandering onto the "wrong" paths. We put wrong in quotation marks because what we offer is just a map based on our experience and we all know that maps can become outdated as the territory changes or less than useful if they contain information that isn't relevant to the goal. (For example, having a topographical map is of little use in navigating the streets of a large city.)

NOT KNOWING WHERE YOU'RE GOING AND WHETHER YOU'RE GETTING THERE; GOING SIGHTSEEING

Frequently we are asked to consult on difficult cases with our colleagues and other clinicians we meet during workshops. Following a brief introduction about the treatment, we typically ask the therapist, "What are your client's goals?" Often, there is a noticeable pause between our question and the therapist's response, indicating that treatment goals are not foremost in his or her mind. This is unfortunate, because if you don't know where you're going, how will you know when you get there? How will you even know if you're headed in the right direction? In the words of a book title we have seen, "If you don't know where you're going, you'll probably end up somewhere else."*

Cul-de-sac #1 — Pursuing the Therapist's Goals

So, if the client's goals are not guiding the befuddled therapist, what is? Sometimes, the therapist's views of what needs to change provide the structure for the sessions. This usually doesn't work too well, since clients tend to view treatment as unsuccessful unless their goals or some mutually negotiated goals have been attained.

Michele observed what was to be a termination session of one of her colleagues from behind the mirror. The therapist was very pleased with the family's progress: The family members were cooperative; they completed all the homework tasks and reported improvement in certain areas. Just as the therapist suggested it might be time to terminate, his clients said, "We have seen improvement in some areas but this has nothing to do with the reason we came here originally." Reviewing his notes after the session, the therapist discovered that, indeed, he had inadvertently gotten sidetracked. He had forgotten the family's goals and was working on his own agenda instead. Although family members polite-

---

*David P. Campbell, Argus Communications, 1974.

ly went along with his plan, they were far from convinced that it was time to stop therapy. Scratching one's arm when the itch is on one's leg does little to relieve the irritation.

Cul-de-sac #2 — Starting With an Unclear Goal

> Problems, whether one calls them *symptoms* or *complaints*, should be something one can count, observe, measure, or in some way know that one is influencing. . . . One of the most important reasons for specifying the problem clearly is so that a therapist can know when he has succeeded. Presumably, when treatment terminates and in a followup interview afterwards, a therapist will want to know definitely whether he has achieved his therapeutic goals. (Haley, 1976, p. 41)

Sometimes the problem is that the therapist never has a clear picture of the client's goal. The goal may be stated in vague terms rather than action words, e.g., "He will have a better attitude," "I will have more self-esteem," or "He will act more lovingly towards me." Since we can't actually see things like attitudes, self-esteem, or love, it's hard for both client and therapist to know when they are happening. It is not unusual, then, for all involved to feel as if they are just going around in circles (because they are).

Cul-de-sac #3 — Losing Sight of the Goal

Assuming that we have a clear picture of the goal at the outset of treatment, we endeavor to never lose sight of it. As our clients talk about themselves, describing their thoughts, feelings and actions, we are continually asking ourselves, "In what way does this [whatever the client happens to be discussing] relate to his or her goal?" Consider the potentially devastating effects experienced by a rock climber scaling the face of a cliff should he get distracted and lose sight of his end goal.

Furthermore, in the back of our minds, we classify the things clients talk about in therapy into three general categories. These categories are: "goal-oriented," "problem-oriented," and "yet to be determined." (Gingerich, de Shazer, and Weiner-Davis, 1988, did some research which closely parallels this perspective of interviewing.)

In the goal-oriented statements, clients talk about the good things they are doing in their lives and their thoughts and feelings about these. Our consistent response to goal-oriented topics is to highlight, amplify, and label the subject matter as newsworthy by showing a great deal of interest and enthusiasm.

When problem-oriented, clients talk about the presenting problem, its history, their understanding of the attending dynamics of the problem, and their hopelessness about the possibility of change. Our response to problem-oriented statements varies. Sometimes, the response is silence, as we listen carefully for positive comments worthy of accentuation. More frequently, we politely acknowledge what they have been saying and gently redirect the conversation to a more fruitful direction. At other times, the problem description is reframed in an unexpected way to see if altering the client's perception of the problem leads to a goal-oriented discussion. If, after reframing, the client again talks about the problem, then this effort is abandoned. On the other hand, if the client responds positively, e.g. "I never thought about it that way; that makes a lot of sense," then we have entered the goal-oriented domain and the appropriate goal-oriented questioning is indicated.

Finally, it is sometimes quite difficult to know if the subject matter being discussed will prove to be productive or not. That is, does the client view what is being talked about as something that will facilitate change or hinder it — or is it simply immaterial? The "yet to be determined" category was created for these times.

When we are uncertain, we wait and listen carefully for clues about the potential usefulness of the point being made. Asking, "In what way will this (whatever is being discussed) make it easier for you to _____ (lose ten pounds, get that promotion, get along better with your husband)?" helps determine the relevance and usefulness of this information. If the client indicates that it will help in some way, we are encouraged. If, on the other hand, our client says that the issue at hand will make it more difficult to accomplish goals, we suggest that it is quite helpful to know what to avoid in order to reach goals rapidly. The discussion can be hastened at this point by saying, "Okay, so that is something that doesn't work for you. What does work?"

There is one final aspect of the "yet to be determined" category. Occasionally clients will discuss a behavior or attitude which seems fairly insignificant to them, but which we see as goal-oriented. Our goal-oriented response, i.e., curiosity, interest and enthusiasm ("That really sounds different from the way you might have handled things two weeks ago!"), usually transforms a neutral statement into a positive goal-oriented one. When this occurs, clients say things such as, "That's true, this really is different. I forgot about what happened two weeks ago."

What is apparent from this framework is the importance we place on remaining focused and on track. We avoid sightseeing if we can help it. Sightseeing, to our way of thinking, is asking about or listening to information which might be interesting or provocative, but which in all likelihood will lead to a therapeutic dead end or a much more circuitous route to a solution.

We once heard a workshop participant ask Steve de Shazer how he resists the temptation of asking clients about
things she considered to be "juicy," since she felt there was a
bit of voyeurism involved in being a therapist. The audience
laughed with recognition. He commented that he no longer
finds those avenues fascinating. Talking about change is
what he finds appealing. We concur.

DOING WHAT HASN'T
PREVIOUSLY WORKED

We initially assume that knowing what is working and
doing more of that will eliminate the difficulty. Certainly,
this is what we emphasize in our work. If, however, things
don't go smoothly, we certainly must inquire about what is
not working, to avoid repeating ineffective solutions.

Dead End #1 — Repeating Past Therapists'
Ineffective Approaches

If our clients indicate that they sought treatment previously, we often inquire, "What was helpful about that experience, and what was not so helpful?" The client's response is
extremely useful information. For example, if we hear, "I
thought my therapist was a nice person, I liked her, but she
just listened to me and never suggested anything or challenged me in any way," we know that this person would be
better matched with a therapist who is directive and active
during the session. Recognizing this helps us meet her expectations and increase the chances of successful outcome.

Similarly, when we hear comments such as, "The therapist told us that we really had a marital problem when we
brought our son to him because of school phobia. We dis-
agreed with that and decided not to return," we know *not* to
tell these spouses that they have a marital problem. For the

time being, issues pertaining to their marriage are probably sensitive subjects, and we would certainly tread lightly in this area.

Obviously, one doesn't have to be a Milton Erickson, or even a therapeutic whiz, to figure out what not to do once you've thought to ask what was negative about prior therapy experiences.

Dead End #2 — Repeating What Your Client Has Unsuccessfully Been Doing to Solve the Problem

One time we observed a session where the therapist asked a mother and her 12-year-old son, "So, what brings you in?" To this, the mother responded, "He never talks to me anymore. I know there must be something bothering him because he got into trouble at school, but no matter how hard I try to get him to talk, he only answers with one or two words. It's really frustrating." After mother's view of the problem was aired, the therapist spent the next 30 minutes trying to get the boy to discuss his perception of the situation. Guess what happened? It is probably no surprise that the boy had little to report; when he did speak, he did so with one- or two-word answers. The therapist felt stuck and this reinforced mother's view of the problem (an unusual joining technique).

Any response other than the one already deemed ineffective has a chance of working. Repeating client's unsuccessful problem-solving attempts during the session or inadvertently suggesting that they do "more of the same" between sessions is devising a plan likely doomed for failure.

Michele had a male client in his forties who had stress-related stomachaches and headaches. Several visits to physicians ruled out the possibility of physical etiology. At the first session this man handed Michele two typewritten pages enumerating the various methods he had employed to rid himself of his ailments. He listed approximately 75 of them. Michele perused them briefly and immediately realized that if she were to suggest a specific technique to eliminate his physical discomforts, the suggestion would then become #76 on his list (this list could be called, "75 ways NOT to cure headaches and stomachaches").

Rather, Michele told him that the discomforts he was experiencing were probably important for some yet unknown reason, and she needed more information about them. She suggested that, instead of allowing himself to think negative thoughts all day long as he had been, he was to set aside a designated period of time each evening for allowing the negative thoughts to spring forth. He was then to discover what he might be able to learn from them. During the second session he stated, "I had a much better week. The strange thing was, the more I tried to have negative thoughts, the harder it became." Although Michele wasn't certain that the intervention would work, she was certain that another suggestion to eliminate the headaches and stomachaches would have been more of the same.

Dead End #3 — Repeating Well-Meaning
Advice and Suggestions of Family Members
and Friends

Generally, prior to beginning therapy, friends and family have offered "helpful" suggestions which have proven to be either ineffective or unappealing for one reason or another. In all likelihood, your client will be as receptive to hearing the same old suggestion from you as he was to hearing it from his friends and family. Conversely, what is often needed to help clients get off dead center is a suggestion framed in such a way that it seems to contradict the same old advice.

If you hear, "You sound just like my wife (my mother, my husband, my boss)," you are in trouble. It is time to switch gears.

NOT ATTENDING TO
CLIENTS' RESPONSES

Often novice therapists intent on perfecting a new therapy model concentrate so hard on saying the right thing at the right time that they forget to carefully observe their clients for verbal and nonverbal reactions. They fail to notice if the client is agreeing or disagreeing, confused, annoyed, or delighted. They just forge ahead blindly, without constantly assessing whether or not what they are doing is working.

No therapy model, technique, or intervention is inherently useful or not useful. It is valuable only if it works. And the only way to know if something works in therapy is to *watch and listen to* people's reactions both during and between sessions. Then, "If it works don't fix it. If not, do something different" (de Shazer, 1985).

Like Milton Erickson, solution-oriented therapists attempt to utilize clients' attitudes about life, relationships, therapy and so on, rather than to persuade clients to replace these views with those that are deemed to be "healthier." Following this dictum, a clear sign that therapy has gone astray occurs when clients disagree with or object to comments or suggestions made by the therapist (unless this is the therapist's intent). If the therapist does not change directions at this point, he risks losing his client or, minimally, impeding the change process. However, it is hard to judge when these critical junctures in therapy occur if you are not watching and listening to your client.

Although seasoned therapists have maps to guide them, they are able to adapt and modify depending on what is occurring during the session. This adjusting and modifying process is similar to the process of a person's chopping wood with an axe. In order to achieve his end goal of chopping the wood into two pieces, he must constantly and intently watch the resulting cut each time he swings the axe. He concomitantly adjusts each swing to give him a clear cut on the log.

One of the dangers of ignoring clients' responses and failing to modify the next therapeutic move is getting stuck. Being "overlyprepared" sometimes creates a rigidity in therapists which hinders rather than helps the achievement of goals.

Several minutes before her next session a therapist asked for some consultation on a difficult case. She had seen a particular family for several sessions and felt stuck. She had developed a fairly elaborate intervention, which she was planning on giving to the family at the end of the next session. Her plan for the remainder of the session was to create a context in which the intervention would make sense. This therapist had her well-defined map.

When the family members entered the room they did not appear to be as "resistant" as the therapist had indicated. In fact, they talked about changes they had made that week. However, since the therapist had her plan, she stuck to it, oblivious to positive comments made by family members. Had she acknowledged the good things that were happening, she would have needed to abandon her "innovative" strategy. She was not prepared to do this. Conversation among family members deteriorated rapidly in the session.

Erickson said it well:

The therapist's task should not be a proselytizing of the patient with his own beliefs and understandings. No patient can really understand the understandings of his therapist nor does he need them. What is needed is the development of a therapeutic situation permitting the patient to use his own thinking, his own understandings, his own emotions in the way that best fits him in his scheme of life. (Rossi, 1980, Vol. 4, p. 223)

REIFYING PATHOLOGY

Problems are not something people have or don't have. How one judges the events in one's life determines whether one has a "major problem," an "interesting challenge," a "small bump on the rocky road of life," or "no problem at all." We believe that determinations about the severity of people's situations are influenced, shaped, and molded during the interviewing process. Therefore, failing to implement certain solution-oriented strategies will undoubtedly reinforce the idea that there really is a problem and that the problem is complex and unmanageable. As we watch others work, we have noticed some therapist behaviors which seem to increase the odds of reifying pathology. We call these "blind alleys."

Blind Alley #1 — Failing to Notice and Amplify Solution-Oriented Behaviors, Statements, and Attitudes

There is a well-known philosophical question, "If a tree falls in a forest, and no one is there to hear it, is there any sound?" Similarly, reports of solutions, strengths and exceptions to the problem pattern which go unnoticed by client and/or therapist seem to dissipate in the air instantaneously. Unless the client labels what he is talking about as important and worthwhile, or the therapist acts in a way that indicates to the client that his topic of discussion is important and

174   *In Search of Solutions*

solution-oriented, the opportunity to create "news of difference" is lost.

Over the years we have grown so accustomed to listening for, asking about, and commenting on anything which might prove valuable in terms of developing a solution that we see an imaginary little red flag waving furiously when these topics are being discussed. We find ourselves thinking, "Find out more about that!" When therapists fail to notice these things, their jobs are made more difficult.

Blind Alley #2 — Failing to Interrupt
Unhelpful Statements or Questions

> How do I know what I think till I see what I say?
> (O'Hanlon & Wilk, 1987, p. 84)

It is during the process of talking about their situations in therapy that most clients begin to crystallize their ideas about the nature and seriousness of their difficulties. Therefore, it is essential that therapists take an active role in encouraging clients to explore solution-oriented topics. Talking about the problem leads to thinking about the problem, which leads to talking more about the problem. Unless the problem is talked about in a new and different way, it will be thought of in the same old way. If thinking about the problem in the same old way worked, your client would not be in your office.

Our view is that talking about things in a certain way often clarifies and crystallizes that particular view. Many people aren't certain of what they think about something until they hear themselves talk about it. Once they do, they tend to think that these are their "true feelings" or real thoughts on the situation.

Part of avoiding the crystallization of problems or unhelpful views is what we call "therapeutic interrupting." It's a bit like an attorney in a courtroom who objects to a line of questioning that may lead in a damaging direction for the client. What we are doing when we interrupt with a comment or a question is making sure that the jury doesn't get swayed in the direction of pathology and intractable problems and that the talk that could crystallize those unhelpful views is not entered into the court record.

Blind Alley #3 — Looking for Resistance

A colleague of Bill's once told him this story. Perhaps it is apocryphal, but it makes our point rather handily. He said that he had been in a psychoanalytically-oriented training/therapy group. He decided to quit the group after he noticed that if someone came late to the group, the interpretation inevitably was that the person was resistant; if someone came early, he was anxious; if someone arrived right on time, he was compulsive. He realized that there was no way to win in this system, except perhaps to leave, which he did!

Occasionally we are all guilty of attributing negative motivations to people's behavior. However, to do so in therapy can have some serious therapeutic ramifications. We do not believe resistance is a real thing that happens during the treatment process. It is simply a label that therapists give to certain client behaviors when a therapeutic impasse has been reached. Unfortunately, labeling our clients as resistant can limit our ideas about possible solutions and cause us to give up using the clients as partners in the change process.

Solution-oriented therapists pay attention to the cooperative elements of the client-therapist relationship and build on these more productive aspects. We no longer "see" resistance because our field of vision is filled with observations of the things that clients are doing to reach their goals and to cooperate with therapy. Focusing on these aspects of the situation usually creates a positive atmosphere in which the therapist is likely to have genuinely warm, positive feelings towards clients and clients are likely to feel the same towards the therapist. This fosters a partnership that can facilitate the search for and implementation of solutions. If clients have objections or are reluctant to follow some course of action, we view these as legitimate concerns that must be dealt with or included in the discussion.

GETTING FANCY

A therapist at the MRI, Lynn Segal, tells a story about a friend that bears repeating here. Lynn's friend knew that Lynn was a competent therapist who was able to help solve even the most difficult problems because of his ability to be clever and strategic in his work. Because of this reputation, the friend asked whether Lynn would offer some advice on solving a dilemma the man was presently experiencing. He was sure that, because of his vast experience dealing with difficult circumstances, Lynn would be able to help immensely. Lynn agreed to try.

The man explained that for the past few weeks the neighbor adjacent to his house allowed his dog to roam freely, which would not have been a problem except for the fact that the dog "deposited" on his lawn. He wondered if Lynn could suggest something really "strategic" to remedy this.

Lynn thought for a moment and responded, "Have you tried talking to him about it, telling him how this irritates you, and asking him to curb his dog?" The neighbor admitted that he had not. Lynn suggested he try that before getting strategic.

In this case, which we mentioned briefly earlier, Bill did a consultation interview with a mother and a daughter who were being seen by a therapist who was participating in Bill's supervision group. When they were asked, neither of them

was quite sure why they had come to the consultation ses-
sion, except for the fact that the therapist had asked them to
come. When Bill asked what had initially brought them to
therapy, the mother reported that the daughter had been
hoarding newspapers. Mother then began to give a detailed
account of the daughter's compulsive hoarding of things
since childhood (she was now in her twenties). Doing a solu-
tion-oriented interview, however, elicited the fact that the
daughter no longer collected and saved newspapers or any-
thing else in a troublesome way. When Bill found this out,
he began wondering aloud why they were in therapy, since
they no longer seemed to have a problem. They were just as
perplexed. Perhaps, Bill suggested, their therapist liked to
hoard clients. The supervisee listening behind the mirror
got the message and began discussing termination with his
clients.

Similarly, one time Michele was asked to critique a marital case study written by a colleague who considered himself
a "problem-focused brief therapist" (Weiner-Davis, 1985).
Early in therapy the goals were defined. Several sessions
later changes were reported that indicated that the goals had
been accomplished. Michele was impressed with the therapeutic skills of the therapist and assumed that the remainder
of the article would be a discussion of his successful approach. Instead, a recounting of many more sessions consti-
tuted the balance of the article. Finally, several months later,
the therapist hesitantly suggested that perhaps therapy was
no longer needed. What was not clear was why therapy continued as long as it did, since the client's goals had been
achieved many weeks prior. Admittedly, the therapist had
forgotten the couple's goals. Furthermore, although he
agreed that the couple had improved, he seemed to hope
that more therapy would solidify the gains made, since he
worried about relapse.

When treatment goals are obtained, if our clients don't say anything, we ask them whether or not it makes sense to stop now. Sometimes clients wish to recontract around a new issue, which is fine. Most of the time clients agree that it is time to terminate. Even when recontracting occurs, we highlight the notion that something has been completed, that they have done what they set out to do. This builds confidence that can help accomplish more goals. When therapy passes the point of goal attainment without the therapist's directing the client's attention to that fact, it appears that the problem is illusive and insolvable (to both therapist and client).

One reason therapists fail to terminate is because, even when there is no longer a problem, clients offer details of their lives which seem to merit intervention — a fight with a spouse, a bad day at work, a ravenous departure from a strict diet, and so on. However, we all know that ups and downs are a natural part of life. Therapy is not meant to be a panacea for all of life's challenges.

9.

Ready, Fire, Aim
Putting Solution-Oriented Therapy into Practice

In the book *In Search of Excellence*, Peters and Waterman summarized the qualities of some of the best companies in America. One of the principles those companies used was taking action and finding out from the marketplace whether their approach was sound or not. They didn't spend a great deal of time doing market research or setting up committees to study matters and recommend courses of action. The authors summed this principle up in a phrase, "ready, fire, aim."

That is what we hope to have you, the reader, do with this book. We have provided what we think is the "ready" part. We have detailed a coherent approach that provides the basis for a successful, respectful way to help people resolve the dilemmas for which they seek therapy. It is up to you to put this approach into practice and to adjust it as necessary, i.e., as your clients teach you it needs to be adjusted—the "fire" and "aim" parts. In order to do this, you need to actually put it into practice, not merely study it in a book.

When Bill first learned hypnosis, it took him some years to master that skill. He read books about it, went to seminars, talked to colleagues about it, read some more, went to more seminars, thought about doing it, read some more, went to more seminars, thought about trying it again, went to another seminar, and so forth, until one day he actually got up the courage to try it with a client. To his surprise, it went pretty well that first time. After that he tried it some more, until gradually he felt as if he knew what he was doing and could get some good results with it in his clinical work.

Some years later, a student came to work at the Hudson Center, where Bill does his clinical work. Her name was Audrey Berlin. Audrey was a bright and enthusiastic student who quickly picked up the style of working at the Hudson Center, where most people do brief therapy and many use hypnosis. When she joined the staff after her internship, Bill was amazed to hear her talk about the things she was doing in therapy within six months of finishing graduate studies. She was doing hypnosis and getting pretty good results; in fact, it had taken Bill many years to get some of the results she was getting. He wondered about it and started paying attention to what she did that was different from what he did. He noticed that when she learned something new, whether from a book or a seminar, she usually went and tried it with one or more of her clients within the next week or so. She might say to her clients, "I learned this new thing this weekend in a course on hypnosis. How about if we try it out?" Many clients were intrigued and agreed. Or she might just go ahead and try the new things she had learned.

Bill realized that there are at least two major styles of implementing new learning—the "Bill O'Hanlon method," which involves a lot of worrying and thinking about what you've learned before you actually try it out, and the "Audrey Berlin method," in which you actually go and try out what you've just learned. Now we don't know which method you'll be using to find out if what we've written in this book works for you as well as we said it does. But we can tell you that Bill has given up the "Bill O'Hanlon method" and is now a committed "Audrey Berliner." Enough said. Now what we'd like to have you do is focus on the times when you've gotten the best results in therapy: What did you do that was different in those cases? How did you get that to happen?

A Conversation
Bill O'Hanlon &
Michele Weiner-Davis

MICHELE   What direction have you taken since the book?

BILL   I've gone in several directions. Most recently, I'm very interested in how spirituality really is a reflection of a solution-oriented approach. I never believed that people were as small as they seemed when they arrived in therapy for help. Small in terms of who they think they are or seem to be—they're not just an anxiety patient or a borderline personality or a depressive.

So my sense of solution-oriented therapy is encapsulated in this idea: we're not buying that this is all there is to the story. Yes, you are depressed. But then, "When aren't you depressed?" And then, "What else is in your life?" There's much more to the story within the person, beyond the person, and beyond people. So I've been really excited about that and the realization that, for a long time, solution-oriented therapy has, for me, had a spiritual basis. So that's one direction.

I think another direction is—

MICHELE   Well, wait, before you go on, I have a question.

BILL   Okay, good.

MICHELE   Talk about how solution-oriented therapy and spirituality intertwine or interconnect for you.

BILL   Well, the two intertwine because in solution-oriented therapy we're always looking for the alternate story, a story that is not so narrowly defined as this person appears to be when he or she comes to therapy for the first time. Every time someone comes in with some main presenting thing I get really curious and think, "Okay, well, when not?" You know, it's like the old Zen story. The Zen master holds up a teacup and asks the Zen student: What is this? The student replies, "I see a teacup." And the Zen master says, "No, if you were really Zen, you would say you see the space inside and around the cup because without those the cup cannot exist." Everyday people see the teacup. The Zen master notices what others don't notice.

I've thought about that story for a long time in terms of solution-oriented therapy. People come in and they say "depression" and I think, well, "What's the space around it and inside it." Within the moments of depression are there moments of notdepression? And outside the depression, if you will, the depressive personality, and the depression, what are the moments that somehow, and in some way, don't get defined by and haven't been defined by the depression. It's a bit like Sherlock Holmes remarking upon the curious matter of the dog barking in the night in the mystery, *The Hound of the Baskervilles.* Watson states that the dog didn't bark. Holmes replies, "The dog didn't bark. That was what was so curious." The dog barked at strangers, so clearly the dog knew whoever came during the night. Holmes noticed what others didn't. I think solution-oriented therapy notices much more of what is there while others often miss so much of what is available because it is easier to focus on the teacup, the problem, the diagnosis, or the personality problem.

So that's the same thing for me in terms of spirituality. I'm often thinking, well, "Where is the person not as small as he or she seems to be?" And what I mean by *spirituality* is when this person goes bigger and gets connected to something beyond the initial story, when he or she goes deeper inside and beyond his or her self and finds connections to other people and also becomes connected to things way beyond people.

MICHELE   So what have you done with this passion of yours?

BILL   Well, I've been teaching about it a lot and I've been writing about it a fair amount. And I've gotten very interested in helping therapists not get so small and so trapped; this is important because these days, because with managed care and litigation, there is all sorts of stuff that worry therapists. I've been saddened in a certain way when I hear therapists say, "Oh, you know, my niece decided she was going to become a therapist and I told her don't go into this field, it's a terrible field." That really saddens me because I was so excited about this field when I first went into it.

   And part of what excited me is that I think that people have a lot of potential and a lot of possibilities. I also think the field still does, even though it is going through some tough times. I've been bringing a spiritual sensibility to people so they have both a sense of individual meaning and a feeling for a bigger purpose that goes beyond just making a living. This spiritual sensibility also can keep their souls alive in this very challenging environment with the litigation, financial worries, and demanding work schedules common to therapy.

MICHELE   And what sort of response have you been getting from people in your workshop?

BILL   Well, a couple of things. I mean, people really do say, "Oh, I really needed this renewal and I needed to remember why I was in this field and why I went into this field and what I'm doing here." They also say, "I need to get out, it's not for me anymore." So that's one thing.

And the other thing is that people, I think, have been surprised that brief therapy has any connection to spirituality. Some people come along and say, "I never would have gone to any workshop that had to do with brief therapy. I just have an antipathy towards it. So I was really intrigued and skeptical when I saw 'brief therapy and spirituality.' I really like spirituality and, now that you say what it is, I like brief therapy. I think it's great." So I think I've been able to bring in a broader group of therapists, a group of people that might have been biased against their cartoon images of what solution-oriented or brief therapy is.

So, Michele, what are directions in which you have gone since the publication of the book?

MICHELE   I've been very, very interested in how to use some of the principles in solution-oriented therapy to help couples make their marriages work. At first, I applied solution-oriented therapy in a traditional way when working with couples but I soon found out that it wasn't just *any* solution that I was after. I was determined to help couples make their marriages more loving so they would want to stay married.

At first, I was a bit ambivalent as to whether it was okay for a therapist to proclaim such a bias in her work, but I found that there were lots of benefits in doing so. The more I gave myself permission to be biased, the more skilled I became at helping couples find solutions within the contexts of their marriages. This led to my becoming more confident and enthusiastic about being a "divorce buster," and I began to notice that my enthusiasm became contagious. More and more couples were leaving with their marriages intact.

And since that time I have been doing lots of teaching of other therapists and inspiring them to become bolder about taking a stand in regard to the benefits of helping couples work out their differences.

BILL   And why couples and why helping them stay together? What's the source of that passion? I mean, what drew you to that and why do you think that's such a crucial area?

MICHELE   When I started doing this, it was in the late 80s and I figured that we had had about 20 years of looking at the results of rampant divorce and disposable marriages. And I think we finally began to figure out that divorce wasn't the simple solution that maybe people thought it was in the 60s. We realized that even in the best of circumstances, divorce often creates new and unintended problems. And I just have the very strong belief that while not every marriage can or should be saved, the vast majority of problems that people are experiencing when they're considering divorce are solvable.

BILL   Right.

MICHELE   And if I can help couples avoid the pain — especially when there are children involved — I'm going to be first in line to do it. And, truthfully, part of my passion is not only due to the fact that it's possible to find solutions to relationship problems, part of my passion comes from my own personal experience. I grew up in a family where after 23 years of what I thought was a perfect marriage, my own parents divorced. Their divorce impacted on me greatly.

BILL   Yeah.

MICHELE   And that certainly lit a fire under me. But it's interesting — back then when I chose that direction, there was precious little research in regard to the benefits of people staying together and avoiding divorce. And now, there is actually some substantial data to back my passion.

It's one of those very rare times in my life when something I'm passionate about may even be right.

BILL   Sorry, I'm going to interrupt you but it sounds like there are two parts to what you've found. And one of the parts, I think, goes back to what we wrote in the book. At the time we wrote this book, many therapists had a delusion that one could do neutral assessments in therapy. And we were pretty clear that wasn't the case.

MICHELE   Right.

BILL   And so I think that one of the things you became passionate about and that you started to articulate when we wrote *In Search of Solutions* is that there is no such thing as neutrality. We both talked about this when we went out and did training initially and then we wrote about this in the book. There is no such thing as neutrality —

MICHELE   Right.

BILL   —when you're doing an assessment in therapy. You always come with a particular point of view, a set of tools, and a set of assumptions. All of these are going to be informing your therapy. And you were just now making that very explicit. I think many therapists are biased *towards* disposable marriages. You see it in the common idea that you can't keep people together if one of them doesn't want to be in the relationship.

And so one of the passions for you is to puncture that myth of neutrality. It just doesn't exist.

MICHELE   Absolutely. I often show this videotape in my
      workshops where a guy is talking about his marriage
      and he's all over the chart in terms of what he really
      wants to have happen.

BILL   Right.

MICHELE   Sometimes he sounds like he wants out,
      sometimes he sounds like he's ambivalent, and
      sometimes he sounds like he wants to make it work.
      And I stop the tape and ask attendees, "How many
      people think he wants out? How many people think
      he's ambivalent? And how many people think he
      wants to make the marriage work?" And in every
      workshop, there are folks in each of those groups.

BILL   Yeah.

MICHELE   And then I have them come up with questions
      they might ask, depending on which group they're
      in, to show how the questions that they ask demon-
      strate the presuppositions that they have in terms of
      their belief about the viability of the marriage.

BILL   Yeah.

MICHELE   This also shows the way in which the con-
      versation would be channeled depending on their
      position.

BILL   Yeah.

MICHELE   I come from the position a marriage is salvage-
      able unless proven otherwise and my questions flow
      from that assumption. So, after I have gathered the
      responses at the workshop, I roll the tape again and
      show the question that *I* asked which, of course, is
      leading in the direction of staying together.

BILL   Right.

MICHELE   And it was very—very simple. I said, "It
      sounds to me from what you're saying that if you
      could figure out a way to get your needs met within
      the context of this marriage, that's something that

you would really like. Am I right about that?" And he replied, "Yes, that's *precisely* what I'm saying." Which, between you and me, wasn't precisely what he was saying. It was part of what he was saying. It was the part I chose to focus upon.

BILL   Yeah.

MICHELE   I focus on the part of people that wants to make their marriages work. And as you and I have talked about before — what you focus on, expands.

BILL   Yes.

MICHELE   So, yes, you're right about that. And in addition to doing the training for therapists that I love to do, it's been very exciting for me to do couple's seminars now. I love getting out there and sharing solution-oriented, marriage-preserving ideas with the general public. It's amazing how resourceful people are in terms of taking the ideas and becoming their own relationship experts.

But let's get back to you, Bill. You started to say that there's another direction you're interested in. Why don't you talk about that.

BILL   Yeah. One of the things that's also worried me after we wrote *In Search of Solutions*, put it out, and then you and I went around the world doing trainings is that people sort of got it confused with some of the stuff that was coming out of Milwaukee. People sort of lumped the two approaches together.

And one of the misunderstandings — either from what we wrote or what was being done by other people in a solution-based way — is this idea of always being positive. Always focus on the solutions. And I had a particular idea in mind when I didn't go in the solution-focused camp and instead cocreated the solution-oriented camp. You and I sat down and watched tapes of each other — of you doing therapy and me

doing therapy—and we talked a lot about it before
we wrote this book and came up with what we shared
in terms of ideas and directions.

One of my adamant ideas is that if you didn't do a
lot of listening to people's complaints, concerns,
problems, and suffering, they probably weren't going
to move into solutions with you. And that to me is
one of the differences between the approach we ar-
ticulated and shared and that of solution-focused
therapy. Someone wrote an article later and joked
that it sometimes appeared to be solution-forced
therapy. That is, the solution-focused model didn't
have any room for people to be negative or complain. Because of that, some clients got turned off
and some therapists got turned off too, I think.

So I started to call what I do *possibility therapy* to
distinguish it from the solution-focused model. In
this approach, you're going to acknowledge the problems. You're also going to orient towards the solutions and open possibilities, and then find out which
of the solutions, resources, strengths, or things that
are working are going to be helpful.

And I started to emphasize a lot more acknowledgment—acknowledgment, acknowledgment, acknowledgment. I think we put this in our book but
it was overlooked. It was a common misunderstanding
partly because other people who were writing about
it focused only on the positives and solutions. Then I
started to get much more interested in an approach
that came out of the idea of acknowledgment and
which derived a lot more from Erickson's work. I
started to find this new approach helpful and I called
it *inclusive therapy*.

So spiritual, possibility, and inclusive therapies are
the directions that have come out of the writing of *In*

Search of Solutions for me. I also continue to try to correct some of those misperceptions that people had and still have about the solutions approach. I don't know whether you've come across that or how you respond to that, but I know the sensibilities in your work and the sensibilities in my work are very similar these days. I'm sure you have made some refinements and additions to your approach since then to distinguish it from what came out of Milwaukee.

MICHELE I totally agree with you about that and I've probably done similar things in different ways. So many of the tapes I show nowadays demonstrate me doing precisely what you're saying.

BILL Right.

MICHELE I emphasize the importance of being present, acknowledging pain, giving people space to talk about their issues. And you're right, a lot of times therapists say, "Wow, I didn't realize that this was part of the model." And so–

BILL Which has been discouraging to me actually. It's like "Oh, you're kidding?" You know someone said, "Well, what happened to Carl Rogers in all this?" And I say well, "That's the first five minutes." If you're not listening to people, how can you ever help them because you won't actually figure out what it is that they're concerned about, complaining about, or suffering with. And if you just move on to "Okay, well, what's going better?," what is really going to get better?

And I like the example that you used before with the videotape. You say, "It sounds like you're not getting your needs met in the way that you like to; but if you could get your needs met within the context of this marriage, that's something you would be interested in, right?" It's just a simple acknowledgement.

It's very, very simple. It doesn't have to take 16 sessions.

MICHELE   Right.

BILL   It's really just a matter of opening the space for the dissatisfaction to move and for people to address what they want — not to focus on the suffering and the complaint but to allow enough room for the negative so that they think "Okay, she's heard it" or "He's understood it and now we can move on." My sense is that some people move right on no matter what you do. But a certain percentage of people will dig in their heels and say you haven't understood how bad their partner is, how bad the situation is, how bad they are, and so on. Until you understand all of that, they think, "I'm going to continue to tell you how bad it is or show you how bad it is."

And so that was an adjustment, I think, that needed to be made for a lot of people. And, again, it wasn't just us in our book who were noticing this. There was a context in which this book and our trainings were happening and we had to, I think, correct some distortions that were happening.

MICHELE   I agree. I'll just give you an example of that in terms of my couples' work. When I'm working with a couple and one person desperately wants to save the marriage and the other one isn't quite so sure, the one who wants to save the marriage usually takes over the session with descriptions of how great the marriage really is and how shortsighted the other spouse really has become.

BILL   Right.

MICHELE   And in other words, they're doing bad solution-oriented therapy. They're dismissing feelings, discounting their spouses.

BILL   Yes.

MICHELE   And as a result, the reluctant spouse becomes
      even more reluctant to focus on any positive aspect
      of the marriage. That's when I split them up and talk
      to each spouse separately.

BILL   Yes.

MICHELE   And when I get the reluctant spouse alone
      and give that person an opportunity to share his or
      her views, feelings, and thoughts about the deteriora-
      tion of the marriage, it's not unusual for this person
      to begin to say, "You know, I've noticed that over the
      past two or three weeks that things haven't been that
      bad, but I didn't want to say this because I didn't
      want my spouse to get his hopes up."

BILL   Right.

MICHELE   And so to me that's a perfect illustration of
      when you provide an environment in which people
      feel understood and heard; it gives them the freedom
      to talk about other parts of themselves.

BILL   I think it does go back to something that I know
      has influenced you, has influenced me, and certainly
      influenced this book—when what you are doing isn't
      working, don't keep doing it. And that's not just a
      guideline for clients. It is for therapists as well. Don't
      get so attached to your method, your theory, your
      idea, or whatever it is that you can't actually notice
      when what you're doing is counterproductive. That's
      something we both do. We tell couples, "Yeah,
      you've got a really good idea there. It's a fantastic
      idea, but did you notice the response as you put forth
      that idea? It just got the opposite of what you
      wanted."
         And I think therapists up to a certain point were in
      that boat – to go back to something we were talking
      about earlier. I think therapists thought when they
      had problems in responses with clients—when cli-

ents weren't changing, patients were changing, or people were resistant or negative—that they just had to do more of what they did all the time. If the person didn't respond, then they were just resistant or an unworkable case.

And I think the revolution that came in with systems therapy, MRI, and the things we were talking about in this book such as constructivism and the solution-based stuff, was if what you're doing isn't working, look to the interactional system. By attending to the system, rather than pointing in one direction and thinking the problem is over there, you begin to consider that the problem may be in the interaction. It may not be, of course, but it often is. Instead of seeing the resistance or the problem being over there or the marriage or the individual being fixed in a certain way, people become very responsive to changes in the context. Even their views about whether they want the marriage to keep going or not can be very responsive to different input and different interactions.

MICHELE   Absolutely. And actually, this discussion about doing more of what works reminds me of another direction I have gone in recently. One of the things that seems to be working in my practice—which flew in the face of the assumptions I had as a rookie therapist—is the value of teaching couples relationship skills. That's not therapy, but marriage education in therapy sessions. I began to notice that when couples were stuck, sometimes a small amount of information about communication or relationships would go a very long way. Couples ate it up. They would go home and put the information to use in their lives.

BILL   Yes.

MICHELE   And what confused me at the time was related
to much of what I had learned from an Ericksonian
perspective — that people don't need relationship
skill-building classes, they don't need classes at all,
and so on. People are complete packages. And it really becomes the task of the therapist to be creative
enough to help people access the resources within.
So I bumbled into something that confused me.

But I reverted to the promise I made to myself
when I became a therapist, which was that I was going to keep my eyes open in regards to the strategies
that seemed to work, the ones that didn't, and approach my clients with these observations in mind.

And that meant abandoning a lot of things that
were once my favorite interventions.

BILL   Right.

MICHELE   And so in this case, I began to experiment a
little bit more with teaching couples skills when it
seemed appropriate. My couples seminars are an out-
growth of this. I discovered quickly that people just
seem to really love these classes, this information. It's
not useful to everybody, by the way. There are some
people with whom you share information and they
just don't use it, and don't seem inspired by it. But
that's true of any intervention or approach.

And so part of what I've integrated in my work
with couples is marriage education. A lot of what I
teach couples during my seminars are Ericksonian-
based tools. However, there is a communication section during the seminar where I teach a more con-
ventional skill — active listening.

BILL   Right.

MICHELE   Now, quite honestly, between me and you,
that's never an exercise that *I* would ever do because

for one thing, my husband wouldn't do it. It just wouldn't fly. But having said that, in spite of my discomfort with structured exercises, many couples report on the seminar evaluation form that it's their favorite part of the day.

BILL   That's great. One of the things we stressed in *In Search of Solutions,* and that I think is coming out in what you're saying, is to individualize things. Instead of having grand psychotherapy theories or grand couples theories, you say, "These are my general assumptions." I'm going to go with them except when they don't work in a particular instance. One of the Ericksonian biases is that people have all the resources they need to make the changes. Now what does that mean exactly? One of the things that people thought that meant was everybody has a solution. All you have to do is evoke the solution. And I would say that's true except when it's not. Which is what gets us to inclusive therapy.

You can start with that Ericksonian assumption. Like you say, "Start with the assumption that the marriage can be saved and that you as a couple can stay together and there is a way to do that." And then you might be proved wrong. But why not start with that assumption? It's the same thing. Start with the assumption they have all the skills and resources they need and then you find that to a certain extent some people actually have those skills and resources. But some people don't. Let's make the distinction rather than lump everybody together in one grand theory and say this is what you do with everyone. This is what you do with most people, except when you don't.

MICHELE   Right.

BILL   And I think the spirit of *In Search of Solutions* was pointing in a certain direction. It's oriented towards solutions and it's oriented towards these assumptions. We also put in the back of the book a story and some warnings telling our readers not to turn this into another formula for what you do *to* or *on* people. You do this *with* people. These are the guiding spirits and principles. But do not turn this into another formula for what you do on people because then you'll lose what you were just saying. We stressed an openness to learning something new and developing something new with this particular individual, couple, family group, or business — wherever you're using this model.

MICHELE   Absolutely.

References

Achterberg, J. (1985). *Imagery in healing.* Boston: New Science Library.

Anderson, H., Goolishian, H., Pulliam, G., & Winderman, L. (1986). The Galveston family institute: Some personal and historical perspectives. In D. Efron (Ed.). *Journeys: Expansions of the strategic-systemic therapies* (pp. 97–122). New York: Brunner/Mazel.

Bandler, R., & Grinder, J. (1979). *Frogs into princes.* Moab, UT: Real People Press.

Bateson, G. (1972). *Steps to an ecology of mind.* New York: Ballantine.

Bergman, J. (1985). *Fishing for barracudas.* New York: Norton.

Birch, J., & Piglet. (1986). Clandestine courage training: Discovered. *Dulwich Centre Newsletter*, Spring, p. 10.

Boscolo, L., Cecchin, G., Hoffman, L., & Penn, P. (1987). *Milan systemic family therapy.* New York: Basic Books.

Burnham, J. R. (1966). Experiment bias and lesion labeling. Unpublished manuscript, Purdue University.

Cousins, N. (1983). *The healing heart.* New York: Norton.

Coyne, J. (1985). Book review of *The process of change* by Peggy Papp, *Family Therapy Networker*, March/April, 60–61.

Deissler, K. (1986). Recursive creation of information: Circular questioning as information production. Unpublished manuscript.

de Shazer, S. (1982). *Patterns of brief family therapy.* New York: Guilford.

de Shazer, S. (1984). The death of resistance. *Family Process*, 23(1), 11–17, 20–21.

de Shazer, S. (1985). *Keys to solution in brief therapy.* New York: Norton.

de Shazer, S., Berg, I. K., Lipchik, E., Nunnally, E., Molnar, A., Gingerich, W., & Weiner-Davis, M. (1986). Brief therapy: Focused solution development. *Family Process*, 25(2), 207–222.

de Shazer, S. (1987). Minimal elegance. *Family Therapy Networker*, September/October, 59.

de Shazer, S. (1988). *Clues: Investigating solutions in brief therapy.* New York: Norton.

Erickson, M. (1966). Advanced Psychotherapy. Unpublished transcript from an audio tape of a lecture.

Fisch, R., Weakland, J., & Segal, L. (1982). *Tactics of change.* San Francisco: Jossey-Bass.

Fish, J. (1973). *Placebo therapy: A practical guide to social influence in psychotherapy.* San Francisco: Jossey-Bass.

Gingerich, W., de Shazer, S., & Weiner-Davis, M. (1988). Constructing change: A research view of interviewing. In E. Lipchik *Interviewing* (pp. 21–32). Rockville, MD: Aspen.

Gleick, J. (1987). *Chaos: Making a new science.* New York: Viking.

Haley, J. (1963). *Strategies of psychotherapy.* New York: Grune & Stratton.

Haley, J. (1973). *Uncommon therapy: The psychiatric techniques of Milton H. Erickson, M.D.* New York: Norton.

Haley, J. (1976). *Problem solving therapy.* New York: Harper & Row.

Haley, J. (1982). The contribution to therapy of Milton H. Erickson, M.D. In J. Zeig (Ed.). *Ericksonian approaches to hypnosis and psychotherapy.* New York: Brunner/Mazel.

Haley, J. (1984). *Ordeal therapy: Unusual ways of changing people.* San Francisco: Jossey-Bass.

Haley, J. (1985). *Conversations with Milton H. Erickson, M.D.* (3 Volumes) New York: Triangle.

Haley, J. (1987). Therapy: A new phenomenon. In J. Zeig (Ed.). *The evolution of psychotherapy.* New York: Brunner/Mazel.

Keeney, B. (1983). *Aesthetics of change.* New York: Guilford.

Lipchik, E. (1986). The purposeful interview. *Journal of Strategic and Systemic Therapies,* 5(1/2), 88–99.

Lipchik, E., & de Shazer, S. (1988). Purposeful sequences for beginning the solution-focused interview. In E. Lipchik *Interviewing* (pp. 105–117). Rockville, MD: Aspen.

Minuchin, S., & Fishman, C. (1981). *Family therapy techniques.* Cambridge, MA: Harvard University Press.

Naisbitt, J. (1982). *Megatrends.* New York: Warner Books.

O'Hanlon, B. (1982a). Strategic pattern intervention. *Journal of Strategic and Systemic Therapy,* 1(4), 21–25.

O'Hanlon, B. (1982b). Splitting and linking. *Journal of Strategic and Systemic Therapy,* 1(4), 26–33.

O'Hanlon, W. H. (1987). *Taproots: Underlying principles of Milton Erickson's therapy and hypnosis.* New York: Norton.

O'Hanlon, B., & Wilk, J. (1987). *Shifting contexts: The generation of effective psychotherapy.* New York: Guilford.

Papp, P. (1984). The creative leap. *Family Therapy Networker,* 8(5), 20–29.

Peters, T., & Waterman, R. (1982). *In search of excellence: Lessons from America's best-run companies*. New York: Harper & Row.

Rabkin, R. (1977). *Strategic psychotherapy*. New York: Basic Books.

Rosen, S. (Ed.). (1982). *My voice will go with you: The teaching tales of Milton H. Erickson*. New York: Norton.

Rosenthal, R. (1966). *Experimenter effects in behavioral research*. New York: Appleton-Century-Crofts.

Rossi, E. (1980). *Collected papers of Milton Erickson on hypnosis* (4 Volumes). New York: Irvington.

Rossi, E., Ryan, M., & Sharp, F. (1983). *Healing in hypnosis*. New York: Irvington.

Rossi, E., & Ryan, M. (1986). *Mind-body communication in hypnosis*. New York: Irvington.

Rouse, J. (1985). Commencement Address. *Johns Hopkins Magazine*, October, 12.

Schmidt, G., & Trenkle, B. (1985). An integration of Ericksonian techniques with concepts of family therapy. In J. Zeig (Ed.). *Ericksonian psychotherapy: Volume II. Clinical applications* (pp. 132–154). New York: Brunner/Mazel.

Stewart, S., & Anderson, C. (1984). Resistance revisited. *Family Process*, 23(1), 17–20.

Suzuki, S. (1970). *Zen mind, beginner's mind*. New York: Weatherhill.

Szasz, T. (1961). *The myth of mental illness: Foundations of a theory of personal conduct*. New York: Hoeber-Harper.

Tomm, K. (1987). Interventive interviewing. *Family Process*, 26(2), 167–183.

Watts, A. (1966). *The book: On the taboo against knowing who you are*. New York: Pantheon.

Watzlawick, P., Weakland, J., & Fisch, R. (1974). *Change: Principles of problem formation and problem resolution*. New York: Norton.

Weakland, J., Fisch, R., Watzlawick, P., & Bodin, A. (1974). Brief therapy: Focused problem resolution. *Family Process*, 13(2), 141–168.

Weiner-Davis, M. (1984). Strategies of motherhood. *Family Therapy Networker*, May/June, 47–48.

Weiner-Davis, M. (1985). Dancing the waltz to rock and roll music. *Family Therapy Networker*, 9(4), 55–56.

Weiner-Davis, M., de Shazer, S., & Gingerich, W. (1987). Building on pretreatment change to construct the therapeutic solution: An exploratory study. *Journal of Marital and Family Therapy*, 13(4), 359–363.

Zeig, J. (1982). *Ericksonian approaches to hypnosis and psychotherapy*. New York: Brunner/Mazel.

Zeig, J. (1985). *Experiencing Erickson*. New York: Brunner/Mazel.

Zeig, J. (1987). *The evolution of psychotherapy*. New York: Brunner/Mazel.

Index

BILL O'HANLON, M.S., has authored or co-authored 21 books and published 45 articles or book chapters. Bill is a Licensed Mental Health Professional, Certified Professional Counselor, and a Licensed Marriage and Family Therapist.

MICHELE WEINER-DAVIS, LCSW, maintains a private practice in Woodstock, Illinois, and is the author of six books including *Divorce Busting* and *The Sex Starved Marriage*. Michele is an Approved Supervisor for the American Association for Marriage and Family Therapy (AAMFT).